New One with My Family

A New Year's Comedy

SHELTON R. JOHNSON

ALSO BY SHELTON R. JOHNSON

Thankful for my Family:
A Thanksgiving Comedy

Merry with my Family:
A Christmas Comedy

Mr. Wilder: A Novel

*Dedicated to all of my immediate and
extended family. I love you all.*

Table of Contents

1 | Daycare

I was really getting sick of this crap. Every time I try to start something, my six-month-old son starts crying. I rushed to flip back over on my stomach and fake sleep. My wife, Tiffany stopped snoring and woke up begging. "Can you please go get him, Stu? I'm so sleepy."

I used the best sleepy voice I could conjure up, "I'm sleepy too."

She argued, "Stop faking sleep, Stu. You were just over here trying to fool around."

I pushed my head up from the pillow. "Huh? How'd you know that? I hadn't even touched you yet."

"I felt you rollover."

"Well if you can feel it every time I rollover, that means that you fake sleep way more often than I do. Plus, it's your turn to get him anyway." My sons cry grew louder as Tiffany smacked her lips and got out of the bed. She removed that wool rescue blanket she calls a nightgown and threw a silk house robe over her shoulders.

Due to nursing, her breasts were noticeably larger. As her husband, I wanted to jump all over her as I watched. But I learned a few months ago that those are just false advertisement for me, and a 24 hour five-star buffet for my son. One night, we had just finished eating dinner and putting the kids to bed. While sitting on the couch, I kissed her and grabbed one. She slapped my hand away screaming, "I'm full! I'm full!"

I said, "I'm full too! We just had meatloaf and mashed potatoes. But that doesn't mean you have to slap my hand away."

She grunted while getting up from the couch. "I'm not talking about my stomach, Stu. I'm talking about my boobs. I need to go pump." I just rolled my eyes and exhaled. I didn't even bother following her to the bedroom. I just laid back and watched SportsCenter. To me, nothing makes a breast look uglier than that thick, plastic, ice cream cone shaped equipment, called a breast pump. I will admit though that as much as I hate those pumps, after I did a price check on formula, I went and bought Tiffany a backup pump. Just in case that one breaks.

The time now is 6:30 AM. I pushed my face back into the pillow to force myself to go back to sleep for as long as I could. With my family and my in-laws arriving tonight for the New Year's weekend, I figured I needed to get as much rest as possible. From the corner of my eye, I watched my wife loosely tie her robe to go nurse our son. That made me feel some type of way because every time she goes into his room, she has on her nice silk robe with cleavage showing. But when she comes to bed with me, she has her head all wrapped up in a bandanna and wears that thick, extra-long nightgown that goes to her ankles. Sometimes I feel like I'm sleeping with an Iranian soldier. Plus, I'm jealous that she gets to walk around the house like that anyway. Angel is almost 18 now, and I can't even leave my bedroom without being dressed like an astronaut. Tiffany always has something to say. "Aren't you going to put a shirt on?" "I can see the top of your boxers." "Don't you think those pants are a little tight? I can see your print."

Either way, now with her out of the room, I squeezed my eyes shut before being startled by my cell phone ringing. I snatched it off the nightstand to see that it was my uncle Al. I figured since he was calling so early, there must've been a problem. "Hey Uncle Al. What's wrong?"

"Boy don't give yourself that much credit. If I had a problem, you'd be the last person I called. Yo' ass couldn't fix a sandwich in a deli."

I ignored his insults. "So why are you calling me at 6:30 in the morning?"

"I was just calling to let you know that me and your Aunt Tammy are going to come up Saturday morning instead of today because my business boomin' down here nephew."

Ever since Uncle Al lost his last job as a mechanic at Southwest airlines last Christmas, he's been referring to himself as self-employed. This is the second time we've talked in the past week, and both times he's mentioned how well this new business he has is doing. It's as if he's wanting me to ask him more about it. But I won't give him the gratification. The last time I asked him about having his own business, I found out he was just selling cigarette singles down at the barbershop.

I rushed to reply so that I could get him off the phone and get back to sleep. "Okay cool. I won't see y'all today, but you'll be here tomorrow. Got it. Thanks Unc."

"Whoa! Hold on boy. Why you talkin' all fast like you're on an infomercial? I got a question. Now what's the agenda for tomorrow when we get there?"

"It really depends on what Angel wants to do since it's her 18th birthday. Pretty much, we plan on hanging out until that night. We're going to head to church at 9:30 PM so they can do the christening of my son before they start the New Year's Eve service. Then we're going to leave there early, around 10:30 PM, so we can head up to DC and watch the ball drop. It's something I've always wanted to do, and I thought Angel might enjoy being in the middle of the city on her 18th birthday night."

"What? You want me to drive all the way from South Carolina to Maryland, just because you want to see the ball drop? Hell, I see two balls drop every morning when I get outta' bed. Matter fact, hold the line. Hold line." I heard a lot of grunting and squeaky mattress springs. "Hey Stu! You still there?"

"Yes Unc. I'm still here."

"Now see there? I'm standing now!"

"Okay. That's good Unc."

"Balls dropped!"

I'd had enough. "I'm about to go Unc. I'll see you tomorrow."

"Whoa! Slow your roll nephew. Don't be rushing me like instant grits. I'ma get off here in a lil' bit. I just wanted to know how my nephew was doing. What's his name again?"

I smiled. "Kendall. He's doing good."

"Yeah that's what I thought it was. I still can't believe you named that boy after a tablet. But I'm glad to hear he's doing good. I can't wait to see him."

"Uncle Al, I did not name him after a tablet. Kendall is a good boy's name. There's been two NBA players with that name."

"Yeah and I bet they both did commercials for Amazon too. Hey hold on Stu. I got somebody beeping in on the other line."

I said, "Okay." but I used that as my opportunity to hang up the phone.

I set my phone on Do Not Disturb. Then I placed it back on the nightstand. The curtains were so thick, I felt like I was in a time tunnel. I couldn't tell if the sun was up or not. They made it easy for me to fall back asleep. Moments later though, my phone rang again. I knew it had to be an unknown number with my phone being set on Do Not Disturb. When I saw it was a 757-area code I perked up. I thought it was an old college buddy from Norfolk State University. I answered the phone barking. That's how I always answered the phone in college.

"Lord have mercy. Boogie, Stu done went and bought him one of those lil' Shih Tzus."

I immediately stopped barking as I heard my Uncle Boogie gasp, "Belle. God watching."

With the Canton Spirituals playing in the background, Aunt Belle smacked her lips. "I said lil' Shih Tzu, not lil' shit at the zoo you ol' snaggle toothed sinner."

Uncle Boogie griped, "Lord have mercy!"

Even though I agreed that a lil' Shih Tzu could easily be considered some lil' shit at the zoo, I was more concerned with why they thought I was a little dog. My voice isn't that high. But more importantly, why are they calling me so early from an unknown number. I decided to focus on the later of two. "Whose number is this? Are y'all stranded on the side of the road or something?"

"Nah we ain't on the side of no road. I'm standing right here in my kitchen watching your uncle drink a beer for breakfast." He belched. "Anyway, this is one of those track phones we use for prescriptions and long-distance calls."

"Prescriptions?"

"Yeah, I know. Your Uncle Boogie thinks the life insurance company done tapped his cell phone. Like they ain't got nothing else better to do than sit up there and listen to him and your daddy complain about gas prices and losing the lottery."

I shook my head. "But Aunt Belle, you know this isn't a long-distance phone call though, right?"

"I don't see how it ain't. I'm down here in South Carolina and you way up there in Maryland."

"I know. But we still have the same area code though. So I'm a local call."

She paused. "Oh."

"So what did you call me for? Are y'all about to get on the road soon?"

"Lord willin' baby. Lord willin'."

"What you mean, "Lord willin'" Aunt Belle? Either y'all about to get on the road or you're not?"

"Nah baby. See I done turned that over to the Lord. I want to come on up there to see y'all. And Lord willin' my bags will be packed and I'll let Jesus take the wheel on up to Maryland!"

"Hold on now Aunt Belle! Hold on! Don't you think that's a little bit much to expect Jesus to pack your bags *and* drive up here?"

"See you one of them new generation Baptists. Ain't got faith in nothing but a toaster oven. Let me tell you about the God I serves – ."

I'm going to spare you all of everything she said. But I will say that by the time she was done, I was so ready to get off the phone I started saying, "Lord willin'. Lord willin'."

In order to get a straight answer to my question, I asked Aunt Belle to let me speak to Uncle Boogie. She complied. With Uncle Boogie getting up in age, he wasn't out in the fields farming by himself as much. He decided to hire some help around the farm and spends a lot of his time communicating what needs to get done and talking with Aunt Belle. So naturally his speaking skills have improved dramatically as of late. But he's still just as loud and country as ever. "Stu! Stu! What's going on with you there boy?"

"Aww man. I can't call it Uncle Boogie. I was trying to get Aunt Belle to tell me what time y'all were going to be up here. All she kept saying was, "Lord willin'. Lord willin'.""

"Yeah I heard her. Sorry about that Stu. Lord willin', I win this lottery! That's what she need to be praying for! I don't know why she be worrying Jesus to death with these little itty-bitty midget prayers. See I don't bug Jesus with no whole bunch of mess. He already busy enough. I keep my prayer life simple. I only ask him for one thing. Lord please help me win the lotto. I'm telling you, nephew. If he help me do that, I promise he won't ever have to worry about hearing from me again. See I'm what you would consider a low maintenance Christian."

I felt like telling my uncle Boogie that his logic may have been a little off. But then I thought, "Who am I to tell him he's wrong? Yesterday I went to a restaurant and asked for a free cup of water with my meal. Then I went to the drink machine and got sweet tea." I asked, "So what time y'all plan on getting on the road Unc?"

"I don't know just yet. How long it take to get there?"

"About eight hours."

"Daggone boy. That's a whole lot of driving. What route you take?"

Oh boy. I really hate when they ask me that question. The only reason I say they is because it seems like every man over 40 doesn't trust the GPS any further than they can throw it. Then they get mad with you for not knowing the roads and just wanting to give them your address. "I don't remember which roads to take Uncle Boogie. But I can give you my address and the GPS on your phone will tell you which way to go."

"Oh hell naw! I don't trust that heffa on the phone! She's liable to have us out there about as lost as a bad Christmas gift. What you take 95 to 64?"

I didn't know what to say. I don't know all those numbers. So I just agreed with him. "Yeah I think so. I usually don't hit any traffic either. But if you just put it in the GPS it will pop right up."

"Boy stop talking to me about that Government Patented Surveillance. I don't want nothing to do with it."

"Um...I'm pretty sure that ain't what it stands for, Unc. But–."

"I don't care! But if you ain't hit no traffic then it couldn't have been on 95. You must've hopped on 85, then got off on 64 to hit 301."

Tiffany tiptoed back in the room. Being careful not to wake Kendall back up, she gently closed the door behind herself before laying on the bed. I answered my uncle carelessly. "Yeah. I guess so." I didn't know what the hell he was talking about with all those numbers. Without ever receiving an estimated arrival time, I rushed to get off the phone with Uncle Boogie so that Tiffany could get some sleep and I could go make breakfast.

After giving her a kiss on the cheek, I crept downstairs to the kitchen. Now I don't want y'all to start thinking I cook breakfast every morning, because I'll whip out a pack of pop tarts in a heartbeat. It's just that I was off work that day and I figured we could all eat a big breakfast together before Angel's birthday since we had no set plans for what we were going to do the next day when the family got in town.

—⌣—

The time was now 8:00 AM and I was hungrier than a diabetic on a diet. The house was filled with the smell of bacon which sat at the center of the dining table. Alongside it was grits, eggs, hash browns, and Belgian waffles I'd prepared as well. Tiffany, who also didn't have to go to work, sat at the table prepared to dig in. She'd even sat baby Kendall in his high chair with his milk and powdered cereal since he could hold his own bottle now. I yelled for Angel to come downstairs and eat. But before I could even finish my sentence, she came zooming into the kitchen. "Hey! Good morning y'all! I could smell the food from down the hall. And everything looks so good." She walked around to give us all a hug and kiss. "I'm sorry I can't stay for breakfast though."

I said, "What do you mean? Your bus doesn't come for another 30 minutes."

"Huh? It's the Friday before New Year's Eve. We don't have school today."

I put my fork down. "What? Y'all out of school again? Boy y'all got more days off than a government employee!" Tiffany and Angel giggled, but I was serious. It's no wonder that she's not learning anything at the public school. They're never open. I remember when we had her private school, there wasn't an excuse good enough. One year, all they had was a two-hour delay on Christmas.

Tiffany raised her hand to block the natural sunlight from getting in their eyes before asking, "So what do you have planned to do today that's stopping you from having breakfast with us?"

"Oh, my friend, Paniquetta about to come pick me up. We're meeting some more friends at IHOP. Then we're going to catch a matinee movie."

I wasn't exactly sure with that name, so I wondered aloud. "Uh… is this Panamanian person a boy or girl?"

Angel rolled her eyes, "It's not a Panamanian person, Mr. Stu. Their name is Paniquetta. And duh, she's a girl."

I put my hand up, "Angel you can stop with all that eye rollin' cause this ain't no duh moment. I got lost with all those syllables in that name."

A car horn honked from the driveway and Angel perked up before looking toward her mother. "Can I have some money?"

Tiffany shook her head and pointed toward me. "You know I don't keep any cash on me. Ask, Mr. Stu."

Angel smacked her lips, anticipating my usual, "No." But because it would be her birthday tomorrow, after she asked I handed her some money from my wallet. "$20! That's it?"

"That's it? Girl you lucky I'm a Christian. I'll snatch that money out your hand faster than I gave it to you."

"You're right. I'm sorry. Thanks, Mr. Stu. But what am I supposed to do with just $20?"

"You can order off the IHOP's low-calorie a.k.a. low-cost menu. Then y'all have enough money to go to the matinee movie and come on back home."

"But what about leaving the tip?"

"The tip? I got a tip for you, don't go! You and Pakistan can stay here and eat a free breakfast. Then sit on the free couch over there and stream all the free Netflix movies y'all want."

"Her name is Paniquetta, and fine, I'll make the $20 work." Angel gave Tiffany and Kendall a hug and kiss before snatching a piece of bacon from the table. She jumped to give me a kiss on the cheek then jetted out the door.

I complained to Tiffany. "Now why did she have to go and grab a piece of bacon? She ain't washed a hand nowhere this morning." Tiffany looked at me sideways to stop talking. "What? Don't look at me like that. I know you saw all that grease that girl had in her head. She ain't put it up there with her feet. Shoot. The girl got more chemicals in her hair than a diesel engine."

"Stu, she can either use the chemicals, or we can pay $200 – $300 every two weeks at a hair salon."

"Nah. I like the way she wear her hair now. It looks good on her." I stood there sipping a glass of orange juice and looking out the kitchen window at Angel and her friend pulling out of the driveway. I smiled and waved at them as I spoke to Tiffany. "That girl's parents need to be slapped for naming her Panic Attack. They know she ain't gonna to be able to get a job."

Tiffany shrugged her shoulders, "I actually like the name Paniquetta. It's original."

"Yeah, and so were donuts at some point in time. But you've never met anybody named Jelly Glazed before, have you?"

"Wait a minute. If you have all that to say about her name, what about Angel? That's not a common name."

"I know, and it wouldn't have been my choice either. That's something you and Roosevelt decided before you met me. But at least with a name like Angel, she has a chance of getting hired by a Christian. Now Pancreas on the other hand, she doesn't stand a chance."

Somehow or another I managed to make Kendall laugh before I picked him up and held him against my chest. Tiffany continued to stare at me like I was senseless as she ate her food.

— ⌇ —

It was nearing 9:30 AM. Tiffany, Kendall, and I were all strapped in the car prepared to leave. Because my in-law's flight wasn't expected to land until 2 PM and my parents were making that hellacious 8-hour drive, Tiffany and I decided to use the earlier part of the day to compare daycare options for Kendall. Up until this point Tiffany had been able to work from home, which allowed us the opportunity to avoid paying for daycare. Recently though, the demands of her career changed and she is required to spend more time in the office.

This is a big deal because daycare options have always been an issue that Tiffany and I disagree on. I believe we should go with the cheapest qualified candidate, simply because it's a daycare. Which means it's their job to watch your child while you're at your job. Period. All that other stuff about teaching them and having great student to teacher ratio means nothing to me. I feel like he can wait until he gets to real school for all of that. Tiffany on the other hand, believes we should put Kendall in a Montessori school. Or as I like to call it, a monetary school. Those prices are higher than Snoop Dogg. I really don't know much else about it. But her and every one else I talked to claims that it will be a great educational start for my son.

We've narrowed it down to two locations. Both are approximately 15 minutes away from our jobs. One is a traditional daycare, and the other a Montessori school. We've decided that we would evaluate them and go with which one "feels" like it would be the best option for Kendall. Which still makes no sense to me because if I "feel" broke then it can't be the right option.

After a car ride full of nursery rhymes and cries for milk, we arrived in front of the Montessori school. It was a long brick building set up like a cheap motel with different colored doors. Because it sat on an excavated 5 acres, it allowed the kids to have an open field to run around and play in. Apparently, it was recess time when we arrived. We parked in front of the sign that read Woody Montessori School. I got out and saw all the kids chasing the teachers around the field. Nothing was organized. All the teachers wore tie-dye shirts. There were random chickens walking around with no coop in sight. Some old guy in the middle was playing an acoustic guitar.

I asked Tiffany, "I know it says Woody Montessori, but are you sure this ain't Woodstock? I've seen less hippies in the 70's caravan."

"Just give it a chance, Stu. Grab Kendall. Here comes our host."

I stood beside Tiffany with Kendall in my arms feeling like I was in the wrong line of work. I wish I could run around a field in tie-dye shirts all day making $1,000 a kid in a school full of children. What happened next though made my jaw drop to the floor. Our host approached us wearing a long teal skirt and holy tie-dye shirt. I'm not talking about the Jesus type holy either. She also bear a nose ring and dreadlocks, which shocked me because I didn't know white people could grow dreadlocks. Black people can't keep nothing to ourselves.

The woman introduced herself as she shook our hands. "Hi. My name is Ms. Etna. I'm the principal here at Woody Montessori." This is when my jaw dropped. I couldn't believe she was the principal. I thought she was part of the grounds maintenance crew. Matter of fact, I was about to give her a compliment on the landscaping before she started speaking.

Ms. Etna walked us to her office, which was really just the only motel, I mean classroom available with adult sized tables and chairs in it. Kendall was quiet and content as I held him. But Ms. Etna suggested, "Mr. Jones, please feel free to let your son play in our toy area while we chat." Tiffany immediately turned to see if that area was clean. I looked over to see if there were any sharp and/or throat sized objects. Afterwards, Tiffany and I looked at each other in an agreement. So I carried Kendall over and sat him on the rubber mat floor in the toy area.

In the play area, I noticed a Hot Wheels playset and regretted my decision to bring him over. Although Kendall can't talk yet, he does make sounds that are embarrassing. For instance, when he's in the bath with his rubber ducky, he will make car sounds like, "Zoom Zoom." But when he plays with his Hot Wheels set at home he says, "Quack, quack." I shook my head and hoped that he didn't notice the Hot Wheels set as I returned to my seat.

— ᔆ —

After sitting through that long meeting where the principal kept bragging about some old Italian woman named Maria, and my son was across the room quacking like a lost baby duckling; it was finally time to go. We told Ms. Etna that we would give her a call if we decided to follow through with Montessori school before attempting to make a swift exit.

Before picking up Kendall, Ms. Etna noticed, "It seems like your child is crawling a bit funny Mr. and Mrs. Jones." Tiffany and I both rolled our eyes and looked at one another. We knew what was going on, but we didn't want Ms. Etna to find out. For some strange reason, ever since Kendall has been able to grab things, he has a habit of stuffing them in his diaper. I told Tiffany that trait comes from her side of the family with Klepto Chris. She denies it.

Either way, Tiffany distracted Ms. Etna by asking about some pictures on the wall while I dug through my son's diaper for Hot Wheels. Once I was done, Kendall and I walked over to where Ms. Etna and Tiffany stood gazing at the picture of the kids in costumes. Ms. Etna explained, "This photo was taken last year during our Halloween celebration." She pointed, "That's my son, Tyler in the Superman costume."

My eyes popped open because her sons costume was two sizes too small. He made Superman look like supper man. I was disappointed though when I looked right next to him and saw the only black kid in the classroom dressed as a rapper. He wore all black with a gold chain, shades, backwards cap, and a microphone made of aluminum foil. He was just grinning his little butt off too. I thought, "His parents need to be slapped for that. Why couldn't they just give that boy a regular superhero or cartoon character costume like everybody else?"

Back in the car, as soon as I closed the door, my phone rang through the Bluetooth speakers. It was my brother, Shane Jr. I answered, "What up bro?" Tiffany cringed. She doesn't like how I talk when I speak to my brother. I whispered to her. "It's either talk like this, or you can get ready for me and Shane to be joking each other for at least 30 minutes before we get to the subject he's calling about." She turned to look out of the window.

"What's up bro? It's about time you answered the phone like you're black. That probably took a lot out of you, huh?"

I smacked my lips and Tiffany giggled. "Shane what do you want?"

"I was just calling to let you know that we on our way. We just got on the road."

"What? Y'all just got on the road? Y'all were supposed to leave like three hours ago."

"I know. But momma and daddy got in an argument, and you know that's going to take at least an hour with his stuttering. Then we stopped by Aunt Belle and Uncle Boogie house just to find out they won't coming."

"What? Aunt Belle and Uncle Boogie ain't coming either?"

"Nope."

I mumbled, "Em. I guess the Lord won't willing."

"Huh? What you say Stu?"

"Oh, nothing. I'll just see y'all when y'all get here."

"Hey! Hold on Stu! Is Tiffany sister, Teresa coming?" I saw Tiffany's head nod so I answered after shrugging my shoulders.

"Yeah. Why? I thought it wasn't nothing going on between y'all."

"It's not. She's my friend on Facebook, but that's about it. But that don't mean that it can't be more. I just needed to make sure that she was coming, or I would've brought one of my baby mama's." Tiffany gasped. "I'm in the mood for spreading some holiday cheer this year bro."

I replied, "Negro, you in the mood for spreading holiday cheer every day. Besides, you're on speakerphone and Tiffany's in the car."

"Come on man! Tell her I was just joking. Her sister don't need to hear about this. I don't be talking to my baby mama's like that no more." I rolled my eyes. "And Stu, why you ain't tell me I was on speakerphone? Now I got to lie to her sister about my baby mama's."

"Shane!"

"Huh?"

"You're still on speakerphone."

"Doggonit! Man bye."

Finally, we'd arrived at Blossom Daycare, the one I wanted. As we walked toward the front desk of the new building, I saw diversity among the parents coming in and out with their children. When I saw Tiffany smiling, I knew that she'd noticed as well. Once inside, we were greeted by a receptionist who wore professional clothes, none of that tie-dye stuff like the other place. After looking around at the exceptional cleanliness of the daycare, I looked up at the security monitor on the wall. It continuously recorded every square inch of the facility. I thought, "It's cheaper, cleaner, newer, diverse, and safer. There's no way we're going with that Montessori school."

The female receptionist who greeted us stood and pointed. "If you guys wouldn't mind taking a short walk down this hallway, you'll see your child's class director waiting for you." I took Kendall out of his carrier and held him against my chest because he was asleep. I love when he sleeps on me. When we turned the corner and saw the obvious class director, because he was the only person in the hallway, I immediately wanted to walk back to the truck. This guy had a permed mohawk and his eye lashes arched. I saw his big, gold, 1994 Mary J. Blidge ear rings from down the hall. As we got closer, I saw his nappy hair that looked like burnt couscous all over his chest beneath a half buttoned pink collared shirt. Before greeting, I smelled a whiff of my grandmother's perfume in the air. He and I clearly lead different lifestyles, but I decided to establish a common ground with the usual black man greeting. "What up bruh?" Followed by, "Are you wearing white diamonds perfume?"

This dude put one hand on his hip and dropped the other one while his wrist was still in the air. "A gentleman never asks, and a diva never tells." He said in a forcefully feminine tone. He looked me in the eye. "Oh, and I don't have any siblings. So, I'm pretty sure I'm not your brother."

My facial expression and thoughts were, "Oh hell naw! I need to know exactly how much time this weirdo is going to be spending around my son." Tiffany reached out and shook his hand that continued to hang in the air while introducing herself. I'm guessing he was expecting me to do the same because he kept dangling it in front of me. I just stood there and looked at him like he was stupid. In my mind I was thinking, "I ain't about to shake no man's hand who has his wrist all folded down like a lady. Dude you have a bone in your wrist. Straighten it out."

An awkward stare took place between him and I for a moment before he gave up and focused his attention on Kendall who remained asleep on my chest. He reached his hand out to touch my son while switching to a baby like tone. It wasn't a far cry from the tone he'd been using thus far. "And will this be the next cute little baby boy under my watch?"

I quickly took a step back and turned my shoulders. "Hey! Get your manicured man hands away from my son." Tiffany and a director both looked at me shocked. I needed to come up with an excuse for my actions fast. "My bad. It's just that my son is sleeping right now and I don't want to wake him. Speaking of watching him, though. Exactly how much time will you spend around my son Mr. Uh...?"

"Knight. Benjamin Knight. You guys can just call me Sweetness though, just like everybody else. I usually spend about two hours per day in each class that I oversee."

I thought, "I know Walter Payton would be rolling over in his grave about this." I said, "If it's all the same to you I'd like to keep our relationship professional, Mr. Benjamin."

He squeezed his lips together like he was sucking on a straw. "Suit yourself."

To me, after Benjamin answered my question, we may as well had left right then and there. Everything said following that went through one ear and out the other. Tiffany wanted to continue with the tour, though. So we went and met the woman who would serve as Kendall's teacher. I can't remember her name, but I do remember her butt. That thing was so big, every time she walked it looked like two hippos playing on a seesaw.

We let Kendall remain in the classroom with the other babies while Tiffany and I went next door to Benjamin's office to discuss the details. This dude's office looked like a five-year-old girl's play house. There were unicorns with butterflies and glittered crap everywhere. I'd never seen more pink and bedazzled items in my life. We all sat down and began to discuss details about the daycare. Tiffany did most of the talking. Suddenly, I heard the national anthem begin to play from the speakers in the ceiling. Benjamin stopped midsentence, jumped up, bent over, and put his hands on his knees. I shouted, "Hey man! What you doing? It's the national anthem!"

He stood up and bashfully placed his hand over his mouth. "Oh. I'm sorry. I thought that was my jam for a second."

I could tell from her facial expression that Tiffany was just as shocked as I was. This grown man, and potential guardian of our son, was about to start twerking it out during the national anthem. I felt so awkward, I didn't know what to say or do. So I just stood there with my hand on my chest until the song was over, like every other normal US citizen. Once the song was done, Tiffany and I remained standing because we were ready to go. Benjamin took that time to explain that the national anthem is played every day at 11 AM to let the staff know that it's lunchtime. I thought, "Well what do y'all do to let them know that lunch is over? A three-volley salute? At what point do you take patriotism too far?"

Either way, Tiffany and I weren't concerned. I interrupted. "Look here, Beyoncé. I mean Benjamin. We're about to leave. We need to stop by the grocery store and run a few more errands. We've seen everything we need to see and we'll let you know if we decide to use your facility."

He stood back up with a grin. "I understand, sir. But you may want to hurry. Positions here do fill fast." At this point, I didn't care if the vacancy was filled faster than a child support application. I just reached out to shake his hand so we could leave. His hands were soft too. It felt like I was squeezing yeast rolls. "Here, let me walk you guys out."

"No. That's so gay." I slapped my knee. "I mean that's okay. I'm sorry. I just seem to be tongue-tied today, but we remember how to get to the front door."

Back in the children's room, I noticed Kendall crawling funny and drooling. Tiffany immediately ran over, picked him up, and used her sleeve to wipe his mouth. I used that time to take one last glance at the teacher's booty. Standing still, it stuck out so far it didn't look like part of her body, almost like a detached garage. Tiffany rushed towards me, placing Kendall in my arms. "Oh my goodness, Stu. Kendall has something else stuck in his diaper." Tiffany dug in his diaper as I held him up.

"Is he wet or poopy?"

"No it doesn't seem like it… Got it!" She snatched a blue marker out of his diaper and raised it in the air with pride. The teacher came over to get it from Tiffany.

"Oh thank goodness. I've been looking for that. I have the cap over there on my desk."

While I watched the teacher walk back to her desk, Tiffany peeked down into Kendall's diaper. Then she looked up at me with bulging eyes and a straight face. I was nervous because I thought she caught me looking at the teacher. I started to blurt out a lie. "I wasn't…"

"Everything is blue."

"Huh?"

"You wasn't what?"

"I… wasn't… expecting… you… to… look in his diaper… for so long."

"I had to so I could see everything."

"No. It's cool. I understand."

"Stu, everything has blue on it. All the way down to his little testicles."

I raised my hand in the air. "Now wait a minute. Don't you think he's a little young to have tested skills?"

"Huh? What? No Stu! That doesn't even make sense. I said his testicles." She could tell from my facial expression that I still had no clue what she was talking about. "His balls, Stu."

"Oh! Why didn't you just say so?"

Tiffany rolled her eyes. "Whatever. His little balls are all blue now."

I shrugging my shoulders carelessly. "Well, I'm sure it won't be the last time."

Tiffany argued. "Stu, this is not the time to be joking. Let's just get back to the car so we can use the wipes to clean him up."

In the grocery store, I struggled to grab the last bag of black eyed peas that just so happened to be placed on the top shelf. I tried everything I could think of to reach them, too. But I kept coming up short, like a midget at a urinal. By this time, I'd already verbalized to Tiffany that I wanted Kendall to go to the Montessori school. Any normal human being would be happy that their child is going to the school of their choice, and that they were able to prove their spouse wrong about something. But not my wife. While I was striving to get to the top shelf, knowing I was afraid of heights, she just stood there with her arms crossed questioning my decision. Tiffany wanted me to explain why I changed my mind so that I can add justification to her theory of me being homophobic.

I explained, "Look Tiff. You know I made the decision because of Benjamin. But it has nothing to do with being homophobic, because I'm not."

"Oh really?"

"Yes really. I don't want my son to be a part of any daycare whatsoever. I would rather have Kendall with me all day so that I can teach him and he can learn from me. Unfortunately, that's not possible because of work and sleep. What's even more unfortunate is that because of work and sleep I only can spend about four hours a day with him. We have an hour before I have to go to work. Then when I get home, we only have about three hours before he has to go to bed. So if you're asking me to choose a daycare out of the limited options that we have, I'm going to choose the one that's closest to sharing the same values and morals that I have. Especially since they'll be around him for eight hours a day, which is twice as long as I have."

"Okay. That makes sense."

"Now I'm not 100% on board with the Montessori school. But I like them a whole lot more than Benjamin. Because I can tell you right now, if I ever saw my son twerking to the national anthem, I would take off my belt and spank him and Benjamin."

Tiffany rolled her eyes and shook her head as a sales associate approached. "Hi. Do you guys need some help?"

I've never been happier to see a pale, frail bodied teenage boy with braces and a bad posture. "Absolutely! I need those black-eyed peas up there." I pointed. That boy put his foot on the bottom shelf and leaped up in the air. He grabbed the bag of peas and tossed them in my hands on his way back down with a smile on his face. I must've looked like I'd just seen a ghost because I was in pure disbelief of what I'd just saw.

The boy looked me in the eye with a confident grin. "I'm a high jumper on the track team." Tiffany and I nodded silently as he walked away. Tiffany's phone rang. She looked at it and smacked her lips.

I asked, "What? Who is it?" She showed me the screen. It was her parents.

2 | FAMILY ARRIVES

Tiffany pressed her cell phone in my chest. "Here, let's trade. I'll take Kendall, and you talk to my dad."

I smacked my lips and grunted while handing over a sleeping Kendall. "Hello."

"Dang Tiffany! You need to take a cough drop don't you?"

"This is Stu, Mr. Frank."

"Oh… Well say so then, son-in-law! And how many times have I asked you to stop calling me Mr.? You're making me feel like I got a job again. Us retired folks don't like that." I could hear my mother-in-law, Nancy, cackling in the background. "So I guess Tiffany's busy taking care of my grandson, huh?"

I looked up at Tiffany with a childish grin. "Actually, we're in the grocery store getting some last-minute stuff and she's standing right here. Do you want to talk to her?" Tiffany turned around and speed walked to the next aisle.

"I know two plus two equals one for some people. But I did call her and not you. That's okay, though. Just relay the message that we're in the rental car now, about to head to your house."

"Okay. I will."

"Oh, and should I take Route 5 or Route 4 to get to your house?"

Before I could even respond I heard my sister-in-law, Teresa, recommending from a distance. "Don't worry about it, dad. I already have the address in the GPS on my phone."

I still took the time to answer Frank. "There is no faster route. Both of them will get you there at the same time. But like Teresa said, if you need help you can just use her GPS."

"Psh, I don't trust her and my wife with directions. Them two couldn't navigate their way down a lit path."

I hung up the phone with Frank, found Tiffany and Kendall, then passed along the message of her parent's whereabouts. Tiffany rushed to the checkout line. "I don't want them out there waiting on us." I followed.

While we stood in line I curiously asked, "Why didn't you want to talk to your dad?"

Tiffany sighed. "It's not my dad. I just know that he would've eventually passed the phone to my mom, and I don't want that headache right now. All she does lately is tell me how she used to parent me. Then if I do anything above and beyond for Kendall, she hits me with her new favorite phrase. *"I don't know what you doing all that for. That boy will be fine."* It almost makes me feel guilty for wanting our son to be better than fine."

I was silent because I agreed with her mother. Just the other day I had to kick out almost $100 on a bunch of bottles and accessories just because it had the name Avent on it. I guess that's supposed to be the Nike of baby supplies. I'm like who cares? When Kendall applies to colleges, the applications won't ask *"What bottles did your parents feed you with his infant?"*

In the car driving home, I looked over at Tiffany who took a deep breath with her head resting against the passenger window. "Look

Tiff, we'll just sit down, have a conversation with your parents, and let them know how it makes you feel. I'm sure they'll understand."

"It's not just that though, Stu. What about this whole weekend? Nobody cares that the baby is going to be completely off schedule. Then who's going to help me clean up after everybody leaves? Oh, and what about sleeping arrangements? Have you thought about where all of these people are going to sleep, Mr. let's invite everybody to stay at our house for the New Year's? I told you this was a bad idea."

I knew whatever I said next needed to be comforting but yet strategically sound. I could tell she was in the mood to dissect any inkling of a lie. I decided to not even address the issue of Kendall being thrown off his schedule because she was right. I also wasn't mentioning anything about cleaning. The only reason she even brought up cleaning is because she wants me to volunteer to help, which I'm not doing. I actually don't mind cleaning, and I used to help her clean all the time, until I noticed her cleaning behind me because what I did wasn't "up to her standards." Ever since then, I figured I may as well be doing something more beneficial with my time, like napping.

I reached over to rub Tiffany's shoulder and stole a page from my mother-in-law. "Everything will be fine. This is a great idea and the perfect time for our families to come together and get to know one another. And yes, I've already handled the sleeping arrangements. So that's one less thing you need to worry your pretty little head about."

Tiffany shrugged her shoulders. "I guess you're right. That's good to know. So where's everybody sleeping?"

Shoot! She called my bluff. I'd given sleeping arrangements about as much thought as moon gravel. "Um, I was going to have my parents sleep in the guest bedroom. Then – ."

"Wait. Why can't my parents sleep in the guest bedroom? They got here first, and they had to travel the furthest."

I didn't care. "Okay. Fine. Whatever. Your parents will be in the guest bedroom. Then my parents can have the air mattress set up in Kendall's room, and Kendall can sleep in Angel's room."

"Hold up. First of all, Angel is about to be 18 and needs her privacy. Secondly, this is her birthday weekend. She shouldn't have to deal with a crying baby all night. I think Kendall should sleep in the bed with us."

As selfish as it seems, all I could picture was me getting no booty this weekend. Tiffany had just made two valid points, though. So I didn't put up any argument. "Well my brothers going to sleep on the flip out couch in the man cave. Your sister can – ."

"Stu, that mattress on the flip out couch is thin, and your brother is a big dude. He won't be comfortable down there. Plus, Teresa can share the bathroom in the basement with my parents since your man cave is next to the guest bedroom."

"Yeah that makes sense."

"Wow Stu. You really were prepared. Good job." I cut my eyes at her. Of course, she would say that after shutting down every idea I had. "So what's going on between your brother and my sister anyway?"

"I don't know. I do know that Shane is interested, but he hasn't seen her smile yet." Tiffany pouted her lips. "Oh don't look at me like that. You know that girl teeth separated like a bad marriage."

"Whatever. I don't think my sisters interested in him anyway. She's picky, and besides not knowing a definite number of how many kids he has, he's a tractor-trailer driver who produces music part-time."

My head snapped back. "So? What's wrong with that?"

Tiffany surrendered her hands in the air. "I'm just saying, the last guy she dated owned three nightclubs in LA."

"Yeah, and I bet she had a tooth in every one of them too." Tiffany deservedly gave me a disappointed stare. I didn't care, though. I was defending my brother's honor. "Look Tiff. My brother is a good dude. If your sister plays her cards right, she might mess around and get upgraded."

"Oh yeah. That's a real upgrade, going from three nightclubs to 18 wheels. And what's the deal with your family and music anyway? Why does everybody feel like they have to be associated with music in some way?"

"What you talking about Tiff? That's not true. I'm not a part of anything musical."

She laughed. "Yes you are! Every book you write always has some silly rap in it." Tiffany began to mock me.

"I'm a writer but I spell things incorrect,
shout out to my homie ABC spellcheck.

I got the whole family bringing in the new year,
but I don't know what time they're supposed to be here.

We got a daughter who's about to turn 18,
she wants money but she can't keep her room clean.

Being daddy makes me want to go and take a nap,
but I can't because my son is always in my lap."

I must admit that I was impressed by Tiffany's freestyle. She stayed in character the whole time and even made me laugh a bit. But whatever smiles I had, left my face and added on to Tiffany's as we pulled up to the house. Frank, Nancy, and Teresa were standing next to a nice-looking rental car parked in the middle of the driveway. I asked Tiffany to stop at the edge of the driveway so that I could stick my head out of the window. "Hey Frank! Can you move your car to the left or right side so we can pull into the garage!"

Frank answered while walking towards me. "Nah! I parked like that on purpose! I don't want nobody touching it! I didn't get renter's insurance on it."

Now face-to-face, I explained. "Frank you don't need renter's insurance. Your regular car insurance will cover you for rental cars too."

Frank rolled his eyes and whispered. "I know that. But like I said, I ain't got no renters insurance."

"What! So you ain't got insurance on your cars in California either?"

He rushed to put his finger over his mouth. "Shh! Don't go telling everybody my business. I don't need insurance in California. I know people."

I pointed. "Well look around, Frank. We're at the back of a cul-de-sac where we are the only black family in the neighborhood. This isn't the bay area where you have to worry about the young black kids flying down here hittin' doughnuts and ghost ridin' the whip."

Frank looked at me in the eyes and smacked his lips. "Psh. The white kids do doughnuts too. Besides, we're talking about a brand-new, blacked out convertible Jaguar F type here, Stu."

"Oh yeah? Well I hope that F stands for free. Because you're going to need all the money you can get if you get in an accident with that thing." Frank waved me off.

"Come on Stu. You just sour that I pulled up in *that*, and not a shiny piece of crap like you had at my house!" I could hear Tiffany chuckle behind me.

"Nah. I would rather you have that shiny piece of crap and insurance so you can park it right."

"All right. Fine. I'll move it since you won't stop complaining about it."

While Frank moved the car, I opened the garage and pulled in. We weren't even out of the car good before Nancy and Teresa came running over to see Kendall. Tiffany and I have gotten used to people not paying attention to us when we have Kendall. So we just let them have their fun, especially since Kendall seemed to be enjoying it from the grin on his face every time his grandmother, Nancy rubbed his cheek.

Frank stood behind Nancy and Teresa with his hands dipped in his pocket. "Wow. I can't believe I have a grandson. It's a doggone shame y'all had to name him Kendall, though."

I thought, "Oh boy. Here he goes." I even saw Tiffany and her mother shake their heads.

Frank went on. "Good thing it wasn't a girl. Y'all probably would've named her Alexa. Lord knows I can't stand that heifer. I bought that Echo and that's exactly what I got, a dang echo. She don't say nothin'!"

Nancy took a break from playing with the baby to join in. "Frank hush with all that lying. The only reason she doesn't say anything back is because you keep on unplugging it, scared that it's going to run up the electricity bill."

Kendall broke up the conversation with a faint whimper while being held in the arms of his Aunt Teresa. Teresa looked down at him and began to rock him up and down while saying, "Shh. Shh." But with each shush his cries grew louder and louder. I personally think it was too much wind on his face coming from the gaps in her teeth. But I didn't say anything. After gripping her breasts, Tiffany grabbed Kendall from Teresa. "I'm pretty full, so he's probably hungry. Plus it's almost his nap time. I'll see y'all in the house." Tiffany walked in the garage entry door. Nancy and Teresa weren't too far behind after I formally greeted them with hugs.

Frank asked me to hang back so that I could help him with the bags. I watched him zip his leather jacket to the top and tug at his Kangol hat. "Stu I don't know how you deal with these Maryland winters. It's colder than a snowman's johnson out here." I looked down at the trunk but was stopped. "Hold on. We'll get to the bags. I wanted to shake your hand, look you in the eye, and tell you man-to-man that I'm glad you decided to stick with your wife and work things out. I know y'all were going through some things the last time you were at our house. But y'all hung in there and made it through, like you're supposed to." I shook Frank's hand and looked him back in the eye.

"Thank you. I really appreciate that."

"See, early on in a marriage is when most of those big arguments happen. Eventually, y'all will be like me and Nancy. Nancy just does lil' devilish, evil crap to get on my nerves, like fry chicken and hide the hot sauce. Connect all the dots on my belt so I can't walk no daggone where. Put on lingerie and go sleep in the guest bedroom. You know, just lil' evil, devilish crap. She put baby oil on the bathroom door knob so I almost pissed myself before I could get in. Had me sitting on the couch all day trying to figure out why she was walking around the house with a towel in her pocket."

I laughed along with Frank. But internally I dreaded having to carry a bunch of luggage in the house. To hurry things along, I suggested, "Come on, let's get these bags so we can get out of this cold." He pressed the bottom of his keychain to pop the trunk and I saw there were only three small duffel bags. That was a pleasant surprise, like getting real wine during communion. In order to expedite things, I went ahead and grabbed all three bags and took them to the guest bedroom in the basement. When I got back upstairs, Frank, Nancy, and Teresa were all standing around the island in the kitchen. They all had their coats off and I was reminded of the long legs and curves Teresa had. She was built like a pair of pliers.

Tiffany came from down the hallway and stood beside me. She smacked her hands together. "All right guys, Kendall is full and napping. Is anybody hungry?"

I said, "Yeah I could eat." Everyone else nodded in agreement. Nancy offered to help Tiffany make some sandwiches and she agreed. Teresa just smacked her lips and patted down her itchy weave. Since it was on my mind, I decided to use this opportunity to rest my hand on Frank's shoulder and apologize. "Hey listen, I just wanted to say I'm sorry again in person that we weren't able to make it to your dad's funeral a couple months ago. I really did enjoy the little bit of time I did get to spend with Mr. George."

Frank looked at my hand on his shoulder, then back up at me. "Look here, Stu. Just because my father was touched by an angel, doesn't mean I want to be touched by man." He yanked his shoulder away and caused my hand to fall off.

Nancy commented, "Well I think y'all so much for saying that. I know I really do miss him around the house calling the 1-800-SEXT lines, hiding naked pictures in his Bible, sitting around thinking of lies to get free Viagra. I'm just really going to miss him."

Nancy's comments were making me feel really awkward, really fast. I interrupted. "I thought he ended up getting married. Why was he still living with y'all?"

Nancy answered. "Oh, he was married. But they lived separate. That lady said he was too much man for her. All he packed for the honeymoon was a scarf, just in case he got cold in the hotel room."

Frank displayed a smile that stretched clear across his face. "Yeah my pop was something else."

I said, "Yeah he was. Did they ever determine what was the cause of death?"

"Yeah. He ended up choking on some tomato soup." Frank said.

Although I never said it, everything about my facial expression screamed, "What the hell?" Nancy added, "You know what they say: When it's your time to go, it's your time to go."

I said, "Apparently."

Tiffany nudged me with her elbow and changed the subject. "What's the box over there on the floor next to the couch in the living room?"

Everyone turned to see what she was referring to before Frank responded. "Oh, that's a gift that Klepto wanted to give the baby. I grabbed it off of the backseat after Stu got all the bags out of the trunk. Teresa can you go grab it for me." Teresa, who'd been playing on the phone this entire time smacked her lips before doing what she was asked. As she got closer I noticed that it was a PS4. I thought that a PS4 was a bit much for a six-month-old boy but I was really grateful.

"Wow thanks for bringing this Frank. I'm going to have to give Chris a call and thank him too."

"Well you better make that call COLLECT or send him a letter because his butt is back in prison again." Nancy said.

Tiffany was just as shocked as I was. "What? He's in prison again? What did he do this time?"

Frank calmly replied. "Come on Tiff. The boy's nickname is Klepto. Even though he's in prison, I'm just happy that he has a job, saved up his money, and actually *bought* something nice for his baby cousin."

I said, "Yeah me too. I didn't know you could earn money in prison, though. You can't even do that in monopoly."

I sat the PS4 on top of the island as Nancy turned around with a large ham and turkey sandwich on a paper plate for Frank. She passed it to him. "Don't worry, it's all gluten-free."

I asked, "What's wrong with gluten?"

Frank looked at his plate with big eyes and rubbed his hands together in excitement. "Yeah! Gluten-free means pootin free for me, Stu. Nancy ain't looking out for me, she's looking out for y'all."

I said, "Well in that case, thank you, Mrs. Nancy." Tiffany and Teresa concurred.

Without warning, Angel busted through the front door, closing it hard behind herself. With her hands in her pocket and a straight face she came stumping through the living room beside the kitchen. "Hi mom. Hi grandma. Hi granddad. Hi Aunt Teresa. Oh, and hi Mr. Stu." Never stopping, she continued to storm down the hallway to her room and slammed the door. I looked at Tiffany and pointed down the hallway towards Angels room. "You see that? If I was her biological father and I didn't have on sweatpants right now, I would take off my belt and – ."

Tiffany lost it. "What the hell is wrong with her! Me and her are going to discuss this right now!" Tiffany went charging down the hallway to Angel's room.

Nancy had one eyebrow raised with a grin on her face. "Discuss? That must be something she read in one of those parenting magazines."

Frank said, "Yeah. That's that new age parenting for you right there. Parents talk to their kids nowadays. These children today actually have a voice. I didn't know I had a voice until I joined the men's choir."

I thought, "Oh boy. They're about to get on one of their never-ending tangents about old-school parenting. Let me get out of here." Even though I agreed with most of it, I just wasn't in the mood to have it preached to me at the time. "Excuse me y'all. I'ma run back here and see what's going on."

Nancy threw both her hands up. "Oh Lord, now here you go!" Although Frank was eating and Teresa was on her phone, I could hear both of them chuckling under their breath as I stared back at Nancy. "First, my daughter just wants to discuss! Now all you want to do is see! I'm not trying to tell you how to parent. But unless you see flesh being hit, it really ain't nothing you need to see. Now Angel is my grandbaby and I love her! But if she ever come in my house like that I would turn her little butt from high yellow to red, to purple, to black, and then back to high yellow again before school so the teachers ain't got no proof."

Frank cosigned. "That's right. And I would reward you with a bag of Skittles when you're done too, honey. After seeing all those colors, you might be in the mood to taste the rainbow."

This time I just turned around and began walking down the hallway. "Hold on, Stu." Teresa shouted as she shot her hand in the air and hopped out of her seat.

I slowly turned around and surrendered both of my hands at chest level. "Look now, Teresa. Me you have already gotten into this before. I'm not trying to – ."

"I know that, Stu. That's why I haven't said anything this whole time. I've already apologized and moved past that. I'm not trying to go back there with you."

"Oh okay."

"I just wanted to know what there is to do around here? Kendall is sleeping, and you, Tiffany, and Angel are about to be in the bedroom. If I wanted to just sit around the house and listen to my parents complain all day I could've stayed in Cali."

"Yeah. You're right. I'm sorry. We have a few museums you can check out. We also have some great hiking trails and fishing spots. I hear that the rock fish are biting this time of year."

Teresa's mouth hung open with her eyebrows squeezed together. "Huh? Stu, I don't do that National Geographic stuff. I'm talking about men, preferably the cute ones with money. That's what I'm looking for."

I pulled my head back in disbelief of what I just heard. "Okay. Looks like I'm going to have to start calling you Thirsty Teresa." Frank and Nancy started giggling.

"No, I'm not thirsty. But I didn't spend a whole lot of money to get my hair done just to sit around the house either. That's a big deal for me, especially since I'm a hairstylist myself." All the laughter stopped. Frank, Nancy, and myself all dropped our heads in an awkward silence. Teresa complained. "Oh y'all know y'all wrong for that."

I said, "Look Teresa, you don't have to worry about a man anyway. My brother is on his way here right now, and I know for fact that he is interested in meeting you."

"Um. That's two thumbs down."

"What?"

"I've seen your brother on Facebook. Don't get me wrong, he's cute and all. But I can't be with nobody who's working at the community center."

"What makes you think he works at the community center?"

"Every time he posts a picture there's a bunch of kids in the background."

I said, "Oh nah. They're his. He's a tractor-trailer driver and freelance music producer."

"Em. Well how many kids does he have?"

I couldn't answer something I didn't know, so I just said, "Look, I'm not about to get into all of his personal details. But when y'all meet I'm sure that's something y'all can discuss."

"Em. I guess."

We heard Angels room door open and we all looked down the hallway. Tiffany stepped out closing the door behind herself. I asked, "So what's the problem."

"It's nothing to worry about Stu. It's really just a female issue. Nothing major."

Nancy butted in. "Well I'm a 60-year-old woman and I never had no female issues that made me come home acting like that. I want to hear a little bit more about this."

Teresa added, "Yeah. Me too."

I threw up both of my hands before another word could be said. "Not me! I'm taking my sandwich to the living room to watch the game."

Frank agreed, "Yeah. Me too."

—⌇—

It was nearing 8 PM when I was awakened by the doorbell. I sat up in the living room recliner. To my right was Nancy and Teresa watching Family Feud on TV. I said, "Oh, that must be my parents and my brother." Teresa perked up, reached for her phone and put on some red lipstick. I was shocked because I've never seen her move that fast. But I guess she figures she has to dress those teeth up the best she can. I turned to my left and saw Frank sitting on the other couch. He leaned forward to put his cocktail glass full of ice on the coffee table next to a nearly half bottle of Crown Royal. I asked, "Why didn't you go get the door Frank?"

He flopped back into the couch and looked up at the ceiling. "I can't lie to you, son-in-law. I'm tore up. I'm not 100% sure I can make it to that front door right now, let alone that bedroom in the basement."

I looked to my right again and saw Nancy and Teresa sitting and shaking their heads. "Where's Tiff and the kids?" I asked.

Nancy answered. "Angel never came out of her room. And Tiff is trying to put Kendall back to sleep because he started crying."

The doorbell rang again. I rose to my feet. "I'll get the door." I walked over and looked through the peephole. "Who is it?"

My mom stood there smiling. "It's your mama and daddy!" My dad raised a stiff middle finger directly in front of the peep hole.

I snatched the door open with my arms extended wide and an uncontainable beam on my face. "Hey! I'm so glad y'all are finally here! I'm so happy to see y'all!"

My mom embraced me with a big loving hug while my dad complained. "You ne-need to a-act like it! He-hell you doing in here? Go-got us ringing the do-doorbell and wa-waiting on the porch like Jehovah witnesses!"

Tiffany came walking down the hallway with Kendall on her chest. "What's going on out here? I'm trying to put Kendall to bed." Then she noticed my parents standing at the doorway. "Oh hi, Mr. and Mrs. Jones. I'm sorry. I should've known it was you all." Tiffany took the time to introduce my parents to her parents and sister.

I interrupted. "Hey ma, where's Shane?"

"Oh, he's out at the car grabbing all our things. He didn't want to have to make multiple trips."

I thought, "Oh boy. They must've brought a lot."

As usual, Kendall stole the show. My parents couldn't get enough of him. Eventually my mom was holding Kendall while standing next to Tiffany. My dad stood a few steps back, next to me, with his hands on his hips. "Gotta tell y-you, son. I-I never would've th-thought I would have a gr-grandson named Kendall. It ki-kind of makes me fe-feel b-bad for canceling my prime membership."

"Dad you know it's not spelled the same, right?"

My mom overheard my comment and jumped in. "Stu when was the last time you heard somebody spell their name when they introduced them self?" I didn't respond.

My dad forgot all about my son's name after he saw Frank's bottle of Crown Royal sitting on the coffee table. My dad is not even supposed to be drinking brown liquor. He reached over the couch and tapped Frank on the shoulder while pointing. "H-hey Frank, you mind if I get me a lil' t-t-taste?"

Frank's head was still in the clouds. "Go ahead. I'm done for the night." My dad almost knocked me over on his way to the kitchen to get a cocktail glass. He filled the glass halfway… with no ice. I think that even made Frank sober up, because he sat up and held his bottle in his lap after that.

I stood in the living room while my dad, Shane Sr., and Frank watched Sanford and son. Although few words were said, I could tell they were becoming cool with one another. I couldn't say the same for what was going on behind me in the kitchen, though. Tiffany stood in the hallway bouncing Kendall on her chest in solitude. Teresa, Nancy, and my mom, Samantha, gathered around the island in the kitchen. All I felt was Teresa laughing from the ancient suggestions my mom and Nancy gave. My mom said, "You know Stu was a music baby, Tiff. All I had to do was sing him some Mahalia Jackson and he would go right to sleep."

Nancy placed her hand over her chest. "Em. You can sing like Mahalia Jackson?"

My dad overheard the conversation and shouted, "He-he-hell naw! More like Curtis Jackson!"

"Dad, Curtis Jackson is a rapper."

He rolled his eyes. "I know."

My mom answered Nancy. "No, I can't sing like Mahalia Jackson, but Stu would fall asleep anyway."

Nancy said, "Tiffany was a book baby. All I had to do was read to her and she would be out like a light."

I told my dad, "She would've never went to sleep at our house then." He nodded.

Nancy continued. "Now Teresa was a pacifier baby all the way. I couldn't get her to stop sucking that thing to save her life."

Out of nowhere, I heard my brother's voice. "Nor should you!" He stood at the front door dropping six duffel bags on the floor as everyone laughed. I walked over and greeted him with a firm hug.

"How long were you at the door?"

He shouted while pointing, "Long enough to hear that she likes suckin'!"

Teresa yelled back. "Liked!... Past tense! And we're talking about pacifiers as a baby!"

He said under his breath to me, "Don't worry. I'm gonna' find out."

I said, "Man come here and let me introduce you to everybody. This is my father-in-law, Frank. Frank, this is my big brother, Shane Jr." Frank looked up, reached to give him a pound, re-clinched his bottle, and went back to sleep. We walked over to the kitchen where I introduced him to Nancy first.

"Hi ma'am. I'm Mop in the Bucket's... I mean Stu's big brother, Shane Jr." She reached out to shake his hand.

"It's nice to meet you. I really like your jewelry. Did you make those pieces yourself? I like to make my own jewelry too, you know."

In true Shane Jr. fashion, he answered. "No ma'am. I'm regular."

Then I extended my arm toward her and said, "Shane, this is my sister-in-law, Teresa."

3 | STORE RUN

Teresa extended her hand with a slight grin. Shane Jr. stretched his arms out wide. "Nah! I've been waiting too long to meet you! Let me get a hug." She leaned in and hugged him with one arm. But Shane Jr. got a few strands of her weave stuck in his mouth. He started spitting and pulling them off of his tongue.

"So, I've been checking out your Facebook page all this time and it never dawned on me that you're a father. How many kids do you have?"

"Got dang! I thought I was standing in a kitchen, not an interrogation room! Look, we just met and you coming out the wood works demanding all the statistics and mathematical equations. Let's get to know each other first and see what happens from there. Numbers really aren't that important anyway. It's all about how you feel your heart."

Nancy mumbled under her breath. "Nah. That could be high blood pressure."

Tiffany interrupted. "Excuse me but I'm about to go try put Kendall back to bed. It looks like he fell back asleep. Do you all want to say good night?" Everyone gave their sweetest farewells to

Kendall as they wished him good night. To return the favor, as a kind gesture Kendall farted.

Tiffany walked down the hallway with Kendall. Shane Jr. refocused his attention on Teresa. "So I heard you're a hairstylist. You must be doing it pretty big to have your own shop." Teresa blushed. "How big is your clientele?" Teresa's blushing stopped. She froze to think of an answer.

"Oh. Well it's like you said, numbers really aren't that important."

My mom stood there smiling while Nancy spoke indistinctly. "This a daggone shame."

I thought, "Look at this relationship being built on lies."

Shane Jr. supported her decision not to tell by slapping her a high-five in the air. "That's right! Numbers don't matter! What's the name of your shop anyway?" Shane Jr.'s contagious smile caused Teresa to smile too. When he noticed her teeth, he jumped back like he'd seen a roach.

"It's called Teresa's House of Style."

Nancy whispered. "It should be called Teresa's Parent's Garage of Clutter."

My mom raised a bag of peas in the air. "Is anybody hungry? I can fry up some chicken and make some rice to go with these black-eyed peas." Nancy's eyes stretched open in shock.

"Wait a minute, Samantha. You can't cook those black-eyed peas tonight. You have to let them sit in some water overnight." I would never say that my mother can't cook. I relied on her meals for 18 years of my life. But I will say that she heavily depends on Jesus in the kitchen.

My mom just waved Nancy off. "Don't worry. Everything will taste fine as long as we say grace." I saw the frustration in Nancy's face so I felt like I had to say something.

"Mom, you can't act like grace is part of the cooking process. That ain't in the recipe."

"It should be! When I get done these peas will be just as tender and juicy."

Nancy was through. She threw both her hands up. "Listen. I'm not hungry. But you all can eat those bullets... I mean peas if you want to. I'm going to bed. Good night everybody."

Everyone wished Nancy a good night as she walked down the basement stairs. Although no one said it aloud out of kindness, eventually my mom was able to tell that nobody wanted to eat what she'd offered to cook. I stood in the hallway watching my mom return the food to the cupboard while Shane Jr. and Teresa leaned on one another shoulders whispering. Shane Jr. stopped everything. "Yo Stu. If her parents are sleeping in the basement, where is everybody else sleeping? Particularly me?" He pointed to his chest which was covered with gold chains.

"Oh, you're going to be sleeping out here on the couch."

"Got dang! You gonna' have me all out in the open like that bruh?" Shane Jr. lowered his voice. "What if she decides to creep up the stairs and get wit ya boy?"

"Well that shouldn't be happening anyway since Tiffany and I are Christians."

"Huh? No y'all ain't! I'm the only Christian in here! Shane Christian Jones Jr."

"What? I'm not talking about your name fool. I'm talking about our religious beliefs and practices in our household. One of them being that there should be no sex before marriage."

"But how can she say something like that when she had a baby before y'all got married? Boy that girl played you like an 8-track."

Teresa butted in. "Look. It doesn't matter anyway. Like you said Shane, we need to go slow and get to know each other first, right? Besides, you got a whole lot of stuff going on with you that I have questions about. So, we have plenty to talk about before we can even start thinking about sex." Shane Jr. turned his back to Teresa, looked at me, and rolled his eyes.

My mom asked. "So where's me and your dad sleeping, Stu?"

"Kendall is sleeping with us so I have an air mattress for y'all set up in his room. And don't worry Ma, it doesn't have a hole in it." My parents and my brother laughed. My mom shouted from the kitchen into the living room where my dad sat comfortably in the recliner.

"Honey! Come on and take out bags to the room! I'm tired!"

"Hell na-naw! I-I ain't grabbing all-all that cr-crap! We only here t-two days, and you-you packed like you h-headed to college!"

"Okay! Don't worry about it! I'll just be sleep when you come to bed!" My dad quickly replied. "L-L-L-Leave those bags a-alone! I-I'll get em'!"

Teresa yelled over to Frank. "Hey dad! Are you going to need some help getting downstairs?" Frank sat up on the couch with his bottle still between his legs.

"Yeah! I guess so. I'm about as tore up as old bank statements." Frank stood on his own while Teresa walked over to help him.

My dad reached out in front of Frank. "Whoa! Whoa! Whoa! Whoa! Yo-you mind if I g-get another t-t-taste?" Frank raised one eyebrow at my dad and spoke with suspicious tone.

"Yeah. Go ahead." My dad grabbed the bottle, and again, filled his cocktail glass halfway… with no ice. Frank snatched his bottle back and studiously held it close to his chest while being escorted down to the basement.

—⌇—

Early the next morning, before the sun rose, I slid out of bed and slowly tiptoed to living room, being careful not to wake anyone. My brother turned to face me. "What's up, Stu?"

I whispered, "Shane what you doing already up? And how did you hear me?" He smacked his lips.

"It definitely ain't for you. I was hoping Teresa would've creeped up those stairs last night. Shoot, I was listening so hard, I could've heard a spider crawling on carpet."

I sat on the floor with my back against the couch where Shane laid. With a devious smile on my face, I asked, "And speaking of Teresa, what do you think about her so far?"

"Well one thing's for sure, you weren't lying about her mouth being jacked up. Her teeth separated like New Edition. She got a nice body on her, though. She's built just like I like, small at the top and big at the bottom… like a slice of pizza."

Suddenly we heard a bedroom door open and close from down the hallway. I turned to see our dad walking toward us in his usual work uniform. He noticed the smiles on Shane Jr. and me. "W-what y'all laughing at?"

I said, "Nothing. We were just talking about Teresa, you know, my sister-in-law Shane trying to get with."

"Yea. How co-could I forget a-all that b-b-b-booty. That girl w-was sure in attendance the d-day that God was h-h-handing out asses."

Shane Jr. said, "Yeah but she was absent on teeth day."

I said, "Yeah she must've called in sick." My dad dropped his head and shook it.

"Y-yall ain't e-ever lied. I n-noticed that t-too. That g-girl t-teeth separated like laundry."

I asked, "And speaking of laundry, how did y'all sleep last night? Did you have enough sheets?"

"Yeah yeah. T-the sheets were f-fine. N-next time though, i-instead of u-using the machine to b-blowup the air m-mattress, use y-your mama's breath. Th-then it'll be heated."

The door down the hallway opened again, and the three of us looked to see my mother coming down the hallway with her hair wrapped, clothed in her nightgown. She didn't come in the living room with us, though. She watched us from the kitchen as she rested her forearms on the island. "Good morning y'all. What are y'all over there smiling about?"

We all said in unison, "Nothing."

"Em. Yeah I bet it's nothing. Hey Stu, where's Tiffany's grandfather, George? I thought he lived with Frank and Nancy."

"Yes ma'am, he did. But I forgot to tell y'all that he died a few months back." My mom sympathized by resting her hand on her chest.

"Aw. I'm so sorry to hear that. How did he pass?"

"He choked on some tomato soup." My mom gasped for air.

"Lord. What in the world." I didn't know what to say so I just repeated what Frank had told me.

"You know what they say: When it's your time to go, it's your time to go."

My dad blurted, "I see!"

My brother said, "Jesus must've gotten tired of waiting on his ass, anytime he died choking on some tomato soup."

I heard the faint creaking sound of another door down the hallway slowly opening. I peeked past my dad to see that it was Tiffany carrying Kendall on her chest. I popped up to wish them both a good morning with hugs and kisses. When Shane Jr. saw my son, he jumped with excitement as well and rushed over to him. "There he is! There's my lil' tablet nephew! Kendall! What's going on with you baby? Tiffany, do you mind if I hold him for a bit?" Tiffany agreed and passed Kendall over to Shane Jr. I tried to instruct Shane Jr. on how to properly carry Kendall. But I was met with smacked lips. "Come on, Stu. Do you know how many kids I have?"

I said, "Um..nah.. not really… I don't." He rolled his eyes.

"Well I have enough to know how to hold a baby. Excuse me." Shane Jr. carried Kendall past me and back into the living room where he sat him up on the end of the couch. Once my son was secure, Shane Jr. backed up. "There you go lil' tablet! Now you sittin' up there lookin' like a grown man! Do you want a beer?" I giggled a little. My mom dropped her head in her hand. Tiffany cringed. But my dad got upset and spoke fluently.

"What? Stu you've been holdin' out? You got beer here?"

The cracking sound of the basement door opening was loud due to its close proximity. Frank, Nancy, and Teresa came up with Frank leading the way. "Hell naw he ain't got no beer here! This is a BYOB weekend." We all laughed and greeted each other before turning our attention to Kendall who remained on the couch smiling, drooling, and using his arms to make himself bounce.

Shane Jr. began to entertain Kendall by placing all of his jewelry on him. "I know what you smiling about lil' nephew! You want my jewelry so you can make your onesie pop! Say no more! Here's my chain… my bracelet… my watch… my shades… and my fitted cap! Now he looks like one of my kids, Stu!"

Teresa politely interrupted. "Um, one of how many?" Shane Jr. played dumb.

"Huh?"

"I'm asking how many kids you have?"

"Oh. I have enough to say that I don't want any more if that's what you asking."

"Okay. But do you have a number?" Shane Jr. threw a fit.

"Lord have mercy! Here you go trying to lock me down with these numbers again! You starting to make me feel like I owe you money!"

While Teresa and Shane Jr. continued to bicker, everyone else in the main living area was enjoying Kendall sitting on the couch in Shane Jr.'s jewelry. They all had their phones out snapping pictures, laughing, and trying to get my son's attention. Tiffany and I just looked at each other and shrugged our shoulders carelessly. The smile on her face made it evident to me that we were mutually entertained by the actions of our families.

Behind Tiffany was the hallway where I watched Angel come out of her room and walk toward us. Tiffany and I greeted her with a quick hug before turning back around to watch our parents. Angel slouched her shoulders and walked into the living room where she stood behind her grandparents. With an optimistic smile, she tapped them both on the back. "Hey. Good morning y'all." Neither Nancy or Frank ever turned around to see her. They both just reached back with one arm for brief hugs and blew kisses in the air. Angel balled her fists so tight they became red. "I'm so sick of this crap! All everybody cares about is baby Kendall! Y'all can't even take the time to tell me good morning on my birthday!" With tears flowing down her face, she covered her mouth and ran to her room. She slammed the door shut behind herself.

The living area was silent as everyone stood in shock. Even Kendall sat still because he could sense that there had been a mood change. Nancy sighed. "Ah. I feel so terrible. I think we should all go and apologize." Frank coughed to clear his throat and raised his hand to speak.

"Um. First off, I don't think *all* of us can fit in that room. Second, we're the grandparents! That means we're old! So we're allowed to forget stuff and blame our age on an as-needed basis. Third, Stu if she keeps slamming these doors, you're going to have to make a trip to Home Depot."

Tiffany rolled her eyes. "Stu, my *mom* is right. We're her parents. We should go in there and apologize to her."

I said, "Um. *We?* I personally think that my family and I should be exempt from this apology. It's hard to remember a day that you didn't participate in. I wasn't at the hospital when she was born. I'm step daddy, Mr. Stu, remember?"

Tiffany said, "Oh. So now you want to claim the step daddy role?"

"Hey, that's what she calls me. It does have its perks. Besides, I need to run to the store and get some eggs for breakfast."

"We have plenty of eggs here."

"I meant grits."

"We have plenty of grits too."

"Did I say grits? I meant bacon."

"We don't need bacon. We bought all of those sausage links, remember?"

"Yeah, but not everybody is a sausage link person, though. Some people prefer bacon. And what about your mom? She doesn't even eat pork." I looked over at Nancy. "Don't worry, Mrs. Nancy. I'll pick you up some turkey bacon while I'm out."

Nancy said, "Oh. Thank you, baby." Tiffany was furious.

"Since when did you not have a problem with buying turkey bacon. What about you always saying, *"If a pig didn't have to die in order for me to eat it, then it's not bacon?"* Or your favorite Sunday morning song, *"That pig was my friend, so drop the bacon in the pan?"* It sounds like you just trying to leave to avoid our conversation with Angel." Even though Tiffany was right, I wasn't going to let her know it. I stuck to my guns.

"Nope. That ain't it. I'm just trying to feed my family."

Tiffany said, "Yeah right."

"Look. I'm going to get dressed and then I'm going. Don't worry. I'll be right back."

Frank shouted, "Hey! Don't leave without me, Stu! And let me tell you something, you got a point about that bacon too. Nowadays these people are getting out of hand with it. I never thought I'd see the day where I have to specify what type of bacon I want. I ordered bacon and the waiter asked me, *"Would you like that to be turkey, Canadian, or traditional bacon sir?"* I looked him dead in his eyes and said, "Oink! Oink! Sucka!"

My brother joined in. "Yeah. Wait for me too. It won't take me long to get dressed."

My dad said, "Me too." Shane Jr. complained.

"Oh boy. If dad is coming, we ain't gonna' get there til' lunchtime. He takes forever to get dressed."

My dad blurted, "I'm ready." Everyone stood there shocked because of what my dad had just said. Shane Jr. questioned him.

"So, you mean to tell me you're going to wear your work clothes on your day off… out of town? Don't you have something a little more stylish you can wear?"

"L-L-Let me tell you something boy. Looking like y-you have a j-job is al-always in style."

Shane Jr. ignored our dad as he began to repeatedly look around and pat himself down. Teresa asked, "What's wrong Shane?"

"I can't find my jewelry. I know I put it on my lil' tablet nephew. But he doesn't have it anymore and I can't remember what I did with it." Tiffany and I nervously looked at each other in the eye. I placed my hand on Shane Jr.'s shoulder and lowered my voice.

"Bro, Tiffany and I have been trying to figure out this little problem our son has been having with sticking things in his diaper."

Shane Jr. shouted. "It's in his diaper!"

He ran over to the couch, picked up a giggly Kendall, and started to undo his diaper. I stopped him. "Shane you got enough kids to know that that's not a good idea. Lay him on his back." Shane Jr. did that, opened the diaper, and found his jewelry covered in white paste.

"What is that stuff?"

Tiffany answered. "Don't try to act like you don't know what that is. With all those kids you have I know you've bought some of that before. All it is is Desitin diaper rash cream." Shane Jr. denied it.

"Nah. I ain't ever bought none of that. All of my kids were Aqua-phor babies. Unless I was going to the club that weekend, then they were Vaseline babies. And if I was planning on leaving the club

with somebody, then they were straight up petroleum jelly babies."
Teresa used a forceful cough to grab my brother's attention. "Oh, I
was just playing. I was just playing." Tiffany fetched Shane Jr. some
baby wipes to clean off his jewelry.

— ᕱ —

When we went to the grocery store, Shane Jr. had my truck smelling
like a nursery after using all of those scented baby wipes to clean his
jewelry. In the passenger seat beside me, my dad pinched his nose
closed and periodically cracked open the window to breathe. He
claimed that he didn't want to leave the window open because it was
too cold outside. Behind him was, Frank. He raised the collar of his
shirt to cover his nose while cutting his eyes at my brother, Shane
Jr. who sat behind me. Shane Jr. sat cool, calm, and collected while
playing on his phone. He's immune to the stinch of a nursery, or
anything else dealing with babies for that matter.

I wondered aloud. "Hey what's y'all thoughts on disciplining a
child? Tiffany and I were talking and I told her that things would be
different with Kendall because I was limited with what I could do
with Angel, being her stepdad and all. She said that's fine, but she
doesn't believe that spankings are necessary. What do y'all think?"

My dad stared back at my brother. "I-it's funny that y-you should
bring u-up discipline. Because I fe-feel like w-whippin' my o-o-oldest
son's ass r-right now." Shane Jr.'s head popped up from his phone to
look at our dad with a frown. "Y-you know I-I never really c-cared
about spanking y-yall, honest. B-back then I-I had too much ot-other
stuff on m-my mind, like bills. One day I-I ca-came home and your
momma t-told me that y-your brother had been c-cutting up in

s-school. I s-sat down, t-talked to him, a-and I-I was done with it. Boy s-she found out and a-ain't give me n-none for f-five days. From t-then on I whipped t-the hell out of y-yall lil' a-asses."

Shane Jr. questioned, "Dang dad! You used to beat us for booty?"

"He-Hell yea. I-I'da done it f-for less than t-that w-with yo' stubborn ass. Hell, one t-time I-I took off m-my belt a-and started whippin' t-the hell out of y-your stuffed a-animals just to g-get her in t-the mood."

Shane Jr. said, "First off, that's messed up dad. Secondly, I don't spank my kids. I just talk to them and hope that they learn. Hitting them only teaches them violence."

My dad replied, "Hell, I-if I were y-you, I wouldn't b-beat my kids e-either. With a-all those kids y-you might mess around a-and tear y-your rotator cuff."

I added, "Yeah, and you better be careful talking to all those kids too. You might need a bullhorn." Shane Jr. sat back in his seat.

"Oh. I see everybody got jokes now all of a sudden."

Although Frank had the bottom half of his face covered with his shirt, I could tell he was laughing. His eyes were squeezed together and his shoulders kept bouncing. I asked, "What do you think, Frank?" He gathered himself before answering.

"You know people can grow up in the same house, have the same parents, go to the same schools, and still be completely different from one another. So I think each child should be disciplined based off of their own personalities. For example, Tiffany never had a problem listening and staying out of trouble at school. So anytime she had a minor slip up, all I had to do was talk to her and she would fix it right away. Now her sister Teresa on other hand, I had to dropkick her ass to get her to act right."

I asked, "Is that why her teeth so jacked up now?" Shane Jr. and my dad busted out laughing. Frank looked offended. I continued to glance at Frank through the rear-view mirror. "Come on, Frank. I know that's your daughter, but you can't tell me that you haven't noticed her teeth." As I parked the truck in front of the grocery store, Frank leveled with us.

"Look, I know that my daughter's teeth are separated like a public-school lunch tray. But she was born like that, honest. Once I got my money right, I offered to buy her braces to get them fixed, but she refused. She said that she'd rather have her teeth look the way that God intended them to."

Shane Jr. blurted, "Don't blame that on Jesus!"

My dad followed, "Yea. God don't like ugly." Frank shook his head.

"Yeah I know. Y'all have no idea how hard it was just to find a dentist who was willing to bring her teeth together."

I said, "Yeah. I'm sure that has to be a lot of miles... I mean money, a lot of money to bring her teeth together."

— ✍ —

Back in the truck on our way home was silent with exception to 96.3 WHUR playing in the background. I couldn't stop thinking about a father that I'd seen in the grocery store. He had a baby strapped to his chest, while pushing the stroller with fighting twins and it, as he walked next to his pregnant wife. Since I received such great advice from them earlier about discipline, I decided to ask for their opinion again. I turned the radio down. "Hey, when did y'all know that you were done having kids?" Before I could even explain my reasoning behind the question, my dad shouted.

"Vasectomy! A-a lil' bit after y-you were born St-Stu, yo' momma and I t-thought about having o-one more. Then s-she gonna' tell me, "*Twins run in my family.*" I said "Hell naw! T-those twins are g-gonna stop r-r-running, sit their ass d-down somewhere, a-and take a-a water break with me. I-I'm through." I g-got my V-vasectomy that week."

My brother, Shane Jr. agreed with our dad. "Yeah. Me too dad. Once I got my vasectomy, I knew I was out of the game." Frank, my dad, and myself all raised an eyebrow while looking at Shane Jr. I went ahead and asked the question that everyone was thinking.

"Um, when did *you* get a vasectomy?"

"My last one was about four years ago."

"Wait, but don't you have a one-year-old daughter? And what do you mean "*your last one*"? A vasectomy supposed to be a one-time thing."

Frank hoisted his hand in the air to interrupt. "Whoa. Whoa. Hold on Stu. Shane Jr., what exactly happened when you went to get your "vasectomy"?"

"First they checked to my ears, nose, and throat. Then they checked my heart rate and blood pressure. After that, it was time for my vasectomy. I pulled my pants down, then the doctor held my family jewels and told me to cough." The chuckle that Frank and I had gradually became a full out laugh. Frank caught his breath between laughter.

"Boy that ain't no vasectomy! Your ass got tested for a hernia!"

My brother said, "Well that explains a lot." My dad held his hand in his head and shook it.

"Boy y-you c-c-can't be my son."

With Shane Jr.'s personality I knew that he wouldn't let that type of attention stay on him for long. "What about you, Frank? When did you know you were done with kids?" Frank sat up in his seat.

"Well hell, since we're all family, and it's not any worse than that story you just said, I'll go ahead and tell y'all. I only got one ball."

Shane said, "Oh hell naw! That's way worse than mine!"

My dad's eyes got big. "Huh?"

Frank explained. "I lost it during a bike accident years ago. That's when I knew I was done."

This wasn't any new information for me. But Shane Jr. had to ask. "Do you mean a bike like a motorcycle that's Harley-Davidson or something?"

"No. I mean a bike like a bicycle, with gay ass pedals and crap. Either way, after I lost that ball I never wanted to have kids again. I was just afraid that with me only having one ball that they would come out half done."

My dad said, "Like a rare steak?"

"Exactly. You know I didn't want the child to grow up only having one eye, one ear, one lip, one ass cheek. Can y'all imagine that? There goes my baby boy going to take a bath with his one ass cheek. And y'all know the other side of his butt is just going to look like an extra wide ass crack. He won't even be able to wipe it good either because he only got one hand."

I pulled into my driveway with tears in my eyes from intense laughter. I noticed my neighbor, Mr. Willis standing on my front porch. He held a plate covered with aluminum foil in his hand. Mr. Willis is a 75-year-old retired firefighter with dark skin, a shiny bald head, and meticulously cared for gray goatee. Before getting out of the truck, Shane said, "Bro. This is a nice town and neighborhood you live in. You got neighbors bringing you food and everything. I might have to bring all the kids up here one day for a lil' vacation."

I said, "Yeah bro. I'm good with that. Just let me know when. I can get you a good deal on a charter bus. I'm sure Tiff won't mind turning the house into a hostel for weekend."

"Aight. bet."

After we got out of the truck, Nancy opened the front door. When Mr. Willis saw her he said, "Good days of grace. Woman you look better than a crispy hundred-dollar bill." I walked on my porch and stood beside him.

"Hey Mr. Willis. This is my family. They came up to visit me this weekend." I introduced him to my dad, Shane Jr., Frank, and Nancy before asking, "So to what do I owe the pleasure?"

While continuing to stare at Nancy, Mr. Willis said, "Well I was over at the house frying some fish and doing some yoga." Nancy's eyes began to flutter. "Then when I got through I said I ain't going to be able to eat all this fish by myself. You know, because I'm single." Mr. Willis winked his wrinkled eye at Nancy before finishing. "So, I decided to bring you over a few pieces for the family, Stu. So they won't go to waste."

Nancy snatched the plate from me as she stared back at Mr. Willis with a huge smile on her face. "You know I used to own a fish fry and yoga studio back in California."

Mr. Willis asked, "Oh, is that right? What was it called?"

Frank shouted from the bottom step. "Her husband's!"

Nancy smacked her lips, turned around, and stomped in the house. Mr. Willis stepped down the stairs to address Frank with a handshake. "I apologize. I didn't know that she was spoken for."

Frank said, "That's all right. Now you do. It was nice meeting you." Then he followed my dad, Shane Jr., and me in the house.

Nancy was leaning against the kitchen counter tapping her foot on the floor with her arms crossed in evident anger from what had just taken place outside. All the men went and sat in the living room to watch TV. I learned a long time ago not to get involved in other people's marriage. So as I put the bag on the counter I ignored Nancy's physical cry for attention and asked Tiffany, "Where is Kendall?"

"He's taking his nap right now."

"Okay cool. Did you talk to Angel?" Tiffany smacked her lips.

"Yes. Me, Teresa, and my mom talked to her. – ."

Teresa, who was sitting on the other side of the island interrupted with a grin. "I hope you're ready to be a step-granddaddy Stu." I wanted to grab a knife out of the drawer.

"What! I'll kill her!"

Nancy said, "Calm down, Stu. Angel's not pregnant. Teresa only said that because usually young wives end up getting pregnant."

I nodded. "Yeah that's true. But wait a minute, though. What does that have to do with Angel? She's not married."

Tiffany said, "But she's engaged to be."

4 | BLACK & MILD

The news was a major letdown. It reminded me of that time I sped to Chick-fil-A because the drive-through line was empty. Then I realized it was Sunday. I verbalized my disappointment. "Oh hell naw! I'll put an end to that crap right now!" Tiffany stepped in front of me and placed her hands on my chest.

"Okay. Calm down, Stu. There's two things that you need to remember here. First, Angel *is* 18 now, so she can make this decision if she wants to. Secondly, even though she seems serious about this, I don't think it's a big deal."

I asked, "What makes you say that?"

Tiffany said, "I was engaged twice before you, Stu."

Teresa said, "I was engaged once before too."

Nancy even added, "I was engaged twice before Frank too." My mother who stood by the stove looked around at the three of them sideways.

"What in the world?"

I said, "Look, I don't know what type of ring collecting y'all got going on in your family. But that ends today! Right here! Right now!" I pointed to the ground. By this time all the men were standing in the living room listening to our conversation in the kitchen.

Frank yelled over. "Hey Stu! It sounds like when you get done with all of this you're going to need a drink! I'll run down to the basement and get my bottle!" My dad tapped him on the shoulder.

"Yeah, l-let me g-get a lil' t-taste of that too i-if you don't m-mind? Just-just a lil' t-t-taste." I watched Frank roll his eyes so hard that his friends back in California could've seen it.

I was trying to get Tiffany out of my way so that I could get to Angel's room when Nancy hollered at Frank. "Yeah that's all you're good for is a stiff drink! It's a doggone shame that my 18-year-old granddaughter has a man willing to marry her who she hasn't done anything for. But the man who I've been with for nearly 40 years, raised his children, cooked his meals, washed his clothes, helped him build his business, and did everything else that a woman does when she loves man, that same man doesn't want to be in a real marriage with me! But every time another man shows interest in me you block him, saying it's for my best interest!" Nancy had tears in her eyes as she spoke from her heart. But Frank didn't care. He stepped away from the basement door to argue.

"I know you ain't talking about that geriatric neighbor that was just on the front porch, are you?"

"As a matter of fact, I am!"

"Okay! Fine! If you want to be with him go ahead! I ain't going to stop you! I just thought you had higher standards than that is all! But if that's what you want to do then go ahead! I don't want nothing to do with you, him, or that fish he brought over! His old behind probably got denture drool all in the batter anyway! Hell, you need to take a peek outside! His near-death ass might not have made it back home!"

"Whatever Frank! Crack your jokes! You just worried that another man might take me from you!"

"No I ain't either. At this point in his life, I'm worried more about his ghost and I am him!"

Tiffany turned her back to me and raised both her hands in the air. "Wait a minute, mom and dad! Mom, what do you mean you're not in a real marriage?" The room was so quiet I could hear my plants growing in the kitchen window. Everyone was standing and looking toward Nancy and Frank. Nancy and Frank stared at each other.

Frank pointed at her. "Go ahead. She asked you."

Nancy shook her head. "Hell no! I'm not about to regurgitate that ignorant crap you thought of, and then tricked me into agreeing with." Frank cut his eyes at Nancy and sighed before turning to face Tiffany.

"Listen, technically your mother and I are married. It's just that legally were not."

Tiffany asked, "So the state of California doesn't recognize you all's marriage?"

Nancy blurted, "Exactly!"

Frank said, "No! Not exactly! The *judicial system* of the state of California doesn't recognize our marriage. But the *people* of the state of California recognize our marriage every day when they see us together with our rings on. See, we've been married, divorced, and made backup. Why should we have to pay all those fees again? You have to pay for the marriage license, divorce lawyer, court fees, alimony, and a bunch of other crap. By doing it this way, we have everything that married people have, and we do everything that married people do. We just don't have the license. Then if she wants to divorce me for somebody else, like she's threatening to do right now, all we have to do is take off our rings, and *boom!* We're divorced! No waking up early for court. No setting up direct deposit for garnished wages. No – ."

Tiffany put her hand up. "Okay dad. I think we got the point."

Nancy said, "Now doesn't he sound ridiculous to you?"

Shane Jr. yelled from the living room. "Hell naw! He sounds like a genius to me!" My brother even walked over to shake Frank's hand. "I respect yo' playa' OG." Teresa cringed in disappointment. But Shane Jr. didn't care as he continued to small talk with Frank.

I tried to erase the last five minutes out of my memory bank as I slid past Tiffany to go to Angel's room. While charging down the hallway, Tiffany came running after me. "No Stu! Don't kill her!" I held her off with my arm.

"Tiff, I'm just going to talk to her. I think she needs to hear a man's perspective."

Frank rushed down the hallway. "If y'all don't mind, there's a few things I'd like to share with Angel to keep her from walking down the aisle."

I said, "Sure. The more the merrier. Let's go."

As I cracked open the door to Angel's room, Nancy yelled down the hallway. "I don't know how you think you're going to help, Frank! You're the last person who needs to be giving somebody marriage advice!"

Frank waved her off. "Woman why don't you hush your mouth! Go sit down somewhere and write a New Year's resolution!"

"If you keep talking slick to me I won't need a New Year's resolution! I'll have a New Year's substitution named Willis!" Once inside of Angel's room, Frank slammed the door shut behind himself.

Before I said anything, I stood there and looked around Angel's room. I knew it had been a while since I'd been in there, but I don't remember it being decorated like this. She had more posters on the wall than a liquor store. Angel was lying face down on top of the covers in her bed. Tiffany and I asked her to scoot over so that we could sit. Frank sat in her desk chair. I said, "Angel, I wanted to come in here and tell you how proud I am of you." Tiffany pulled her face back as she gasped for air in shock.

Frank said, "Whoa. Whoa. Hold on now, Stu." I raised my hand to interrupt.

"No. No. Just hold on, Frank. Let me finish. Angel I'm proud of the young woman you've become and all the smart choices you've made in your life up to this point. That's why I'm so upset about you making this bad decision to get married right now." Angel quickly looked up at Tiffany.

"OMG mom! You told him?"

Frank quickly butted in. "Them. I know too… Hell, we all know."

Tiffany said, "Yes. I told Stu and everyone else overheard me."

Frank cut in again. "Don't you think he needs to know? Who's going to pay for the wedding?"

Angel said, "Me and my boyfriend don't need any money. All we need is love. Besides, we plan on getting married at the courthouse and taking our honeymoon in St. Maarten."

Frank had to catch his breath from laughing to ask, "Well who do you think is going to pay for the trip?"

Angel pouted her lips. "Wait a minute. My fiancé told me that the government pays for whatever honeymoon we want to go on after we get married."

I mumbled, "Boy, it sounds like y'all going to need some sense to go with all that love." Tiffany nudged my arm to stop, but she had her head turned laughing.

Frank said, "Angel, maybe you should look at your mother as an example. She graduated from college and had a career before she went stupid and got married. But at least her and Stu were able to afford the nice lifestyle you're accustomed to because of it. In fact, your mother was so smart, she graduated as a Viking in her class." Angel's eyes grew with excitement.

"Wow! Mom you never told me you used to be a Viking!" Tiffany smacked her lips.

"That's because I've never been a doggone Viking. Dad what are you talking about?" Frank's eyes were pushed together in confusion.

"I thought you were picked to give that long ass speech at your graduation because everybody said you were the smartest." I looked up at the ceiling to keep from laughing while Tiffany spoke.

"You're talking about valedictorian. Yes, Angel I was selected as valedictorian of my class. That doesn't mean I was a smartest, though. That just means I had the best GPA."

Frank extended his arm. "See there, Angel. Your mother was smart enough to drive a car that got the best gas per adventure." Angel started laughing.

"GPA doesn't stand for gas per adventure, granddaddy. It means – ."

I interrupted. "Forget all that! Does this boy have a name?"

Angel said, "Yes. Everybody calls him Ratchet."

Frank said, "Well that's good. At least he has a job. With a name like Ratchet he has to be a mechanic."

Angel said, "No. He's not a mechanic. People ask him that all the time though for some reason."

I said, "I'm not about to call somebody Ratchet who's not a mechanic."

Tiffany told me to calm down. "Stu, his real name is RaQuanilius." Frank and I both scratched our heads.

I mumbled, "I spoke too soon. I'll call him Ratchet."

Frank asked, "So how did he get the nickname, Ratchet?"

I started talking trash until I was interrupted by, Angel. "I don't care nothing about how he got his nickname, Frank. All I know is if he shows up around here, I'm going to whip hi – ."

"He's a UFC fighter, granddaddy. Ratchet is the name that he fights under." Angel blurted out during the middle of my rant. Her comment made me change my whole ending.

"I'm going to whip...him... up some... eggs and bacon, so we can discuss why two young people like yourselves would want to rush into such a major commitment?"

Frank poked his lips out in disappointment of my response. Angel jumped up to hug me. "Oh wow! Really, Mr. Stu? One of the questions I wanted to ask you guys was if I could bring him over to introduce to you guys! He said he would've asked you for permission to marry me. But he was afraid you would've said no because he's 21 without a steady source of income, living in a studio apartment with his cousin who sells dope. But it's okay, though. Ratchet says with his undefeated record of 13-0, he should be fighting for bigger purses soon, especially since he's in the heavyweight division."

I bit down on my lip like it was a smothered pork chop. I was trying my best not to speak out of emotion. Tiffany put her hand on my shoulder. "Wow Stu. I'm surprised to see you respond to all of this with such a level head. I figured you would've got more riled up." I wanted to put a run in her stocking for that comment. What does she expect me to say? One of the joys of being a father to a girl is intimidating her boyfriends. Now I'm the one that's intimidated. Tiffany said, "So what else did you want to ask us? You said that was only one of the things."

"Oh yeah. Remember when you guys said that you weren't planning anything for my birthday, but if I thought of something that I wanted to do I could do it?"

I said, "Yeah."

Frank turned his back to everyone and looked toward the ceiling. I heard him mumble, "If these ain't the dumbest two parents living. Lord have mercy."

Angel resumed. "Well I know what I want to do. All of my friends are going to Club Love tonight in DC and I want to go too. Can I?"

I said, "Wait a minute. Ratchet isn't going to be at this club too, is he?"

"Oh, no sir. It'll just be my girlfriends. Paniquetta is driving."

"Okay. I just wanted to make sure that nobody was trying to make love in Club Love."

Angel's face scrunched in defense of him. "No. Ratchet isn't like that at all. Y'all just don't understand him. What we have is real and special. He knows that I am waiting until marriage to have sex."

Frank shouted. "Bingo! That's the reason right there. No wonder that boy wants to rush to get married."

I agreed. "Yeah. As a matter of fact, let me see your engagement ring. I bet it's fake." As Angel handed me her ring she argued that Ratchet told her that the diamond was real. After seeing the ring, I thought, "Technically he's right. The diamond is real…real small. I've seen bigger rocks in a fishbowl."

Tiffany asked, "How can you tell the difference between a real and fake diamond, Stu?" I explained the breath test.

"A real diamond sheds fog almost immediately. But a fake diamond will hold fog for a few seconds."

Frank said, "Are you sure we should use your breath, Stu? I mean, we want to *test* the rock, not melt it."

"I know you ain't talking. At least I'm up for the job, Frank. With your old weak ass lungs, you'll have to pump your inhaler on the ring." After Frank and I went back and forth with each other for a while, I did the breath test and found that Angel's diamond was a fake. Angel was heartbroken. I thought, "Dang. This boy can't even afford to buy a big fake diamond." Angel rested her head on her mother's chest. Tiffany wrapped her arms around Angel and patted her on the back in consolement.

Like any young woman in love, Angel cried out. "The ring might be fake – ."

Frank interrupted. "That ain't no might sweetheart. That ring is definitely fake. Trust me! If that thing didn't want to shed Stu's breath, something is definitely wrong with it." Angel closed her eyes and wiggled her head in frustration.

"Okay! Fine! Whatever! The ring is fake! But his love for me is real! This doesn't have anything to do with sex either!" Frank gave up on trying to convince Angel otherwise as he surrendered both his hands in the air. I gently grabbed Angel's hand and stared into her tearful eyes.

"Angel, I know it hurts hearing this, but it's the truth. A lot of times young men and teenage boys mistake lust for love. One of the reasons your mother and I raised you in the church is so that you could learn what real love is. I suggest you take a step back and evaluate if this young man loves you like the Bible says he should." Angel sat silently to let what I said sink in before agreeing.

Tiffany asked Angel. "What about your brother's dedication? How would you make it to that if you're going to the club?"

"Oh. That won't be a problem. His dedication is at 10 PM and that will take about an hour. Then I'll leave right before pastor starts his New Year's sermon, which puts me in the middle of the Club Love dance floor at 11:30 PM." Angel was snapping her fingers and rhythmically moving her shoulders with a smile on her face and her tongue hanging out.

I was so bothered by the thought of her being in the middle of a nightclub without my supervision, that I didn't know what to say. The only thing that came out was, "Hey! Put yo' tongue back behind your teeth and stop the happy!"

Tiffany asked, "Stop the happy? Is that even English? What's wrong with you, Stu?"

Angel added, "Yeah. It's my birthday. I'm supposed to be happy."

I said, "Angel we all know it's your birthday. Chill out. You done already had 17 of them."

Frank sat with his bottom lip poked out in digust. "Em. Y'all said y'all raised that girl in the church, and tonight she's going to leave service early to go to a nightclub?"

Tiffany said, "We're not any better, dad. We're leaving service early too so we can go see the ball drop."

"We? Don't try to make me the scapegoat for your sins. Y'all are members down at the church, not me."

— ✍ —

Tiffany continued to argue with her dad while Angel drove her mother's car to pick up Ratchet. Only the sound of Kendall whimpering after his nap made her give up the debate and leave Angel's room. I wasn't too far behind her in Angel's doorway when Frank grabbed my right shoulder. I turned around. "What's up, Frank?"

"Hey. Look here, Stu. This been on my mind ever since last night. Your dad seems cool and all. You know, good peoples, good peoples. But I gotta tell you, if his stuttering ass asks for another t-t-t-t-taste of my liquor, he's going to have to ch-ch-ch-chip in."

Walking back to the kitchen I glanced over at the living room where my dad sat in the recliner watching TV. Next to him, on the couch closest to the kitchen, I saw the back of my brother and Teresa's heads. They sat shoulder to shoulder, while looking down giggling. I interrupted my mother and Nancy in the kitchen as they cleaned up after breakfast. "It looks like they're finally starting to connect a little bit, huh y'all?"

My mother said, "Yes. New love is such an exciting thing."

Nancy agreed. "Yes, it is. I remember when I first started dating, Frank. I would be so anxious to hear from him all day. Then when he came around me I would get butterflies."

Frank walked up behind me and released a roaring five second belch. He pointed at the three paper plates on the island, each having a bacon, egg, and cheese sandwich on it. "Are one of these mine?"

Nancy was irritated. "Yes! Now grab it and carry your nasty self to living room to eat it!" While Frank walked away with his plate, my mother and I held our noses in disgust. Nancy continued, "I'm sorry about that. But like I was saying; when he used to come around I would get butterflies. Now he comes around I get butter knives just to keep his gross behind away."

As I reached out for my sandwich, my dad walked up behind me and placed his hand on my shoulder. "What's up dad?"

"C-come on out t-to the g-garage. I-I-I need to t-talk to you." I had no idea what he wanted to talk to me about. I took two quick bites of my sandwich and followed him out to the garage. Neither one of us had remembered to grab our coats, and since the temperature was so cold I figured we wouldn't be outside long. But I figured wrong. If my dad's stuttering problem wasn't enough, the cold weather made his teeth chatter. I stood there with my arms crossed trying to stay warm while he kept repeating himself. "I j-j-j-j-j. I j-j-j-j-j." I put my arm around him, hoping my body heat would help. It was like warming up an old car.

"Come on dad. We can't be out here all day."

"I know. I j-j-just wanted to t-tell you I'm proud o-of you as m-my son and a-as a father t-to Angel and my l-little e-reader grandson, Kendall. I-I see you g-getting' frustrated though, son. Y-you know y-you ought to train a-a child in the w-way they should go-." I finished his sentence.

"So that when they are old they won't depart from it. Yeah, I know that, dad. That's why I'm so frustrated. I'm trying to train them in the right way but they're just not getting it. My son likes to use his diaper to shoplift, he makes crazy sounds only when people are around, and he slaps his female teachers on the butt. Then when Angel isn't having a mood swing, she's off somewhere getting engaged." My dad admirably looked up at me with a smile.

"You st-still don't understand. D-don't g-get so f-focused on the training part t-that you become f-frustrated. L-L-Look at the s-second part of t-that scripture. It s-says "*when they are old*" t-they won't d-depart from it. Y-you're looking for perfection n-now, a-and it ain't g-going to happen. B-but they're l-listening and w-watching, though. Ju-just enjoy these t-times. One d-day you'll look b-back on t-them and laugh."

"Thanks dad. I really needed to hear that."

I truly took heed to what my dad said. I felt more relaxed walking back in the house until I heard Tiffany scream. I went running in through the garage door, down the hallway toward Tiffany. She stood there with her back to me and Kendall's head lying on her shoulder. Kendall bobbled his head up to look me in the eye, then burped up some of the milk he'd just ate on my brand-new Redskins slippers. Now I wanted to scream. My dad had a smile on his face as he pat me on the shoulder to walk past. "W-When they're old, s-son. W-When they're old." Tiffany turned around with her eyes fiercely squeezed together.

"Stu. We need to have a talk in our bedroom *now*!"

In the bedroom Tiffany sat on the bed with Kendall. I leaned against the dresser and glanced down at the milk on my slippers as she pointlessly pat Kendall's back to burp him. "What's wrong, Tiff? Why are you screaming and stomping to the bedroom?"

"Your brother has to leave."

"What? I'm not kicking my brother out! What do you want me to do that for?"

"I just saw him and Teresa on the couch beside each other laughing while he was rolling up weed! He has to go!"

"Hold on! He ain't going nowhere. Shane wouldn't do that...here. How are you so sure that ain't your sister's weed and she just don't know how to roll up?"

"I know that ain't Teresa's weed because she can't afford no weed!"

"Dang. She can't even afford a nickel bag?"

"Nope. Not even a nickel bag."

"Em. I guess she didn't get the memo that the recession is over yet, huh?"

"No. Don't start teasing, Stu. My mom said that she hasn't had a client in her shop in over four months."

"I don't know why y'all keep calling it a shop. It's your parent's garage."

"It's a shop because that is the place where she does her client's hair."

"No. It can't be considered a shop if you walk in there during the winter and you have to keep your coat on."

"Whatever, Stu. We both know that my sister can't do hair well. But what are you going to do about your brother?"

"Like I said, I know Shane wouldn't do that…here." A light bulb went off in my head. "You know what? I bet you any amount of money that Shane was probably just freakin' a Black & Mild." Tiffany looked up at me nearly cockeyed in confusion.

"What the hell is that?"

"Whoa Tiff! So we're cursing around our chirrrn' now?" I pointed toward Kendall.

"No. No we're not. But he's just a baby. So he doesn't understand what I said. Besides, that wasn't intentional. It was a reaction out of shock."

"Yeah, and that's the same thing I said when I found out you ate the last row of my Samoas Girl Scout cookies. You dogged me for a whole week about that."

"OMG Stu. Can you stay focused? Let it go. Move on."

"Okay. I'ma stay focused. But I'll say this; if our son keeps hanging around you, his first word will have four letters in it." Tiffany didn't even dignify my comment with a response, just an impatient stare.

"Anyway, "Freakin' the Black & Mild" is when you take the clear plastic lining out of the cigar. In order to do so though, you must unwrap the cigar and take the tobacco out. Now when you roll the tobacco back up in the cigar paper, it can appear as weed to the untrained eye because it's the same technique, just a different substance. People do this because they believe the clear plastic lining in the Black & Mild is what causes cancer." Tiffany's mouth hung open in disbelief.

"But that's so dumb. Why would somebody believe that when chewing tobacco has no plastic in it and still has a cancer warning on the can?"

"Listen Tiff, if you're asking me to explain this dumb logic, I can't. As a matter of fact, I wasn't there when it was created. But I would bet money that whoever came up with that idea was higher than Cheech and Chong on a space shuttle. All I know is that hood people believe hood myths, which causes what we have right now, hood activity. It even has a hood name, "Freakin' the Black & Mild." I guess "Pulling the Plastic" wasn't good enough."

"What about your brother, though?"

"I'll talk to him and tell him to do it in the car. Even if it isn't weed, it's not something he should be doing in our living room."

Without warning we heard Nancy yell from the kitchen. "Sit down! Just go sit down!" Tiffany and I jumped up and ran to see what was the matter. In route I could hear the bickering between Nancy and my mother, Samantha. I saw them both standing in front of the stove.

I forced myself between them yelling, "Hey! Hey! Hey! *Stop*! What is going on?" Nancy reached across me to point at my mom.

"Stu, your mother is trying to bake sweet potato pie and she hasn't even boiled the sweet potatoes! She just sprinkled some cinnamon and nutmeg on the sweet potatoes, put them in that rock-hard frozen crust, and tossed it in the oven!"

I said, "What?" Nancy opened the oven.

"Yes. Look at that lumpy crap."

My mother argued. "Those potatoes will melt and that pie is going to taste so good."

I shamefully dropped my head and lowered my voice. "Mama, you know that rolls are your thing. Every family dinner we've had, you do the rolls. Why you trying to do all this extra stuff at my house?" She tried to answer me but I didn't let her. "No. No. Mama please just do the rolls."

My mother slapped the oven mitts down on the stove and crossed her arms. "Fine! I guess I have time to find somebody to do my hair now since I don't have to cook until dinner."

As Nancy used the mitts to pull the "pie" out of the oven, Teresa jumped up from the couch. "I can do your hair for you, Mrs. Jones!" Everyone in the house looked down at the floor like it was a group prayer. My mother didn't know any better, though.

"Sure. That sounds good to me. I have all my products in my room. So do you just want to do it in there?" Teresa agreed and followed my mother to her room.

I walked over and sat next to Shane Jr. on the couch. Before I could even get adjusted in my seat, Frank looked over at my brother and requested, "Hey let me get a hit of that when you're done."

Shane Jr. replied. "I got you." Then he looked over at me. "What's up baby bro? My lil' tablet nephew doing aight?"

I said, "Yea Shane. Kendall's fine. I came over here to tell you that I'ma need you to take that outside bro. I know it's only tobacco and you're not smoking it in the house. But it doesn't look good and it's not something that we want being done in our house."

Frank cut in. "Speak for yourself, Stu. It looks good to me." My dad cackled in amusement.

Shane Jr. blew up. "Lord have mercy! I should've known Stu runs his house like basic training! Boy I had more freedom than this on house arrest!"

Frank butted in. "Dang, Stu! I didn't know you were so square. It's too cold outside to be freakin' a Black & Mild. The only thing he's going to want rolled up out there is a blanket."

Shane Jr. was on his way to the garage door when a loud, thundering, police-like knock came from the front door. Tiffany walked toward the door with the baby. "Oh, that must be Angel and her fiancé."

I shouted. "No! Back up! Angel has a key and she doesn't knock that loud." I looked around. "Is anybody expecting anybody?" Everyone shook their heads no.

Nancy perked up. "That might be Mr. Willis coming back for his companion… I mean container."

I disagreed. "No. His knocks are a lot lighter and weaker, especially in this type of weather."

Frank looked at Nancy. "So, you're saying his knocks are almost near-death type knocks, huh Stu?"

"Yeah. Something like that." Shane Jr. walked with me to the front door. But he stopped midway to put his Black and Mild down, like that was going to turn him into Mike Tyson all of a sudden. I peeked through the peephole and shook my head with a chuckle. I yanked the door open and threw both my arms out. "Roosevelt Rogers!"

5 | LOVE IS BLIND

Roosevelt threw up both his arms. "Stu! What's up with you?" We dapped each other up and I invited him in. Roosevelt looked up at me. "Stu, I don't know how many times I have to tell you, you can just call me Ready." I grinned.

"And Roosevelt, I don't know how many times I have to tell *you*, that I'm not." Roosevelt and I laughed before I introduced him to my brother and my dad. Frank stood there with them, and the three of them looked at us like we just robbed the police. I asked, "What y'all looking at us like that for?"

Shane Jr. said, "I ain't ever seen two baby daddies get along before." Roosevelt brushed him off.

"Oh, it ain't ever been like that between me and Stu. We reached an understanding from the beginning and been cool ever since."

Shane Jr. said, "Em. Well that's good for y'all. All my baby mama's new baby daddies don't like me, even the ones I don't know. One time I went to the barbershop and I didn't know that one of the new baby daddies work in there. Man that dude took my hairline back to Africa."

The five of us chatted for a bit before my dad and Frank went back to the couch. Shane Jr. went to the garage to finish freakin' the

Black & Mild. Roosevelt and I walked over to the kitchen where he immediately noticed Tiffany holding Kendall. "Oh, is this the little baby, Nook. He's a handsome little boy. I was going to ask if it's a family name or something?"

With agitated tone I said, "No. Nook is not a family name, and Nook isn't his name. His name is Kendall."

Nancy mumbled. "I don't know what you're getting all upset for. It ain't like it's a big difference."

Roosevelt pulled a small metal car out of his pocket. "Hey look what I have for you little Nook... I mean Kendall. It's a Hot Wheels car." My son smiled.

"Quack! Quack!"

Roosevelt looked back at me in confusion before turning to face Kendall again. "Um. No. It's zoom! Zoom! It's a fast car Kendall."

My son insisted with his dimply smile. "Quack! Quack!" Roosevelt gave up and handed the toy over to Kendall. Of course, my son looked at it for all of two seconds, then forced it down his diaper.

Roosevelt said, "He must be saving it for later, when he can get on the floor and really play with it." I just went along with it.

"Yeah. I guess so."

Tiffany said, "I'm surprised to see you, Roosevelt. You didn't tell anybody you were coming."

Roosevelt tried to throw a little slick comment in. "Hopefully it's a pleasant surprise." Tiffany shut it down.

"No. It's more like a plain old, pointless, I really could've done without this type of surprise." The smile left Roosevelt's face. He scratched his head to think of a response.

"Speaking of surprises, I did text Angel when I was about 15 minutes away. She told me that she wouldn't be here when I got here, and that she was excited to see me. She even said she had a surprise for me too."

Nancy yawned, "Yeah. The diamond surprise." Roosevelt blushed. "Oh wow. Come on now y'all. She didn't have to do that for me." Tiffany said, "Don't worry. She didn't."

The door opened from down the hallway as my mom came in the kitchen to desperately grab a bottled water out of the refrigerator. With her hair wrapped, I asked, "How's it going back there?"

"It's hot back there. We decided to take a break so I could get some water and Teresa could go twerk on a black millionaire, or something with your brother."

I said, "Mama it's freak a Black & Mild."

"Whatever. Teresa's doing my hair good, though. She doesn't want anybody to see it until it's done, including me. That's why I have this wrap on. Y'all don't have any mirrors back in that room either. That's okay, though. It feels like she's doing the same thing my hairdresser back home does." I wanted to see underneath that old, cotton, slavery-like hair wrap my mom was wearing so bad. But I exercised self-constraint.

As I introduced Roosevelt to my mother, Tiffany passed Kendall over to me. "Here, Stu. My arms are starting to hurt." Both my mother and Nancy looked on adoringly as I bounced Kendall to get him to settle.

My mother moaned. "Aw. That's so sweet. I'm so proud of y'all working together to raise that baby. That's the way it's supposed to be."

Nancy agreed. "Yes. Even with all those years of raising Angel, you three have amazed me. The reason I say three is because it's rare that you see blended families who get along with the biological parent *and* raise a good child. Believe it or not, my only advice would be for you all to continue to pray for your family." My eyes grew in shock. "I know it's hard to believe because I will curse you out in a hot minute. But every night those girls lived under my roof I prayed for them."

I wanted to ask, "So that means you're still praying for Teresa then, huh?" But I didn't say anything.

My mom said, "The only advice I would give is that you both come to accept the fact that Kendall is a boy, and boys come with *different* issues than girls. Girls are more emotional. Boys are more physical. You won't be able to raise them the same. Even if they were the same sex you wouldn't be able to raise them the same because no two children are alike, even if they have the same parents. Just love them both the same. Be fair. But just know that each of them will present their own challenges."

Tiffany and I received their advice with gratitude. I asked, "Hey ma. All I did was hold the baby for Tiffany. What made you consider that to be great co-parenting?"

"Em. That's more than your daddy ever did. The only time he held y'all was when he was giving y'all a spanking so y'all wouldn't run away."

My dad yelled from the living room. "T-T-T-That's the o-o-only time I'm supposed to!"

Nancy yawned a second time. "Look, you all. I'm about to go take a nap. I got up early this morning and I think I have a case of that jet snack too."

Tiffany interrupted. "Mama, I think you mean jet lag, unless you just finished eating a bag of pretzels."

"Whatever it is, I'm tired. Listen, Samantha. I know we had our little disagreement earlier, but do you mind cooking a pot of spaghetti for everyone? It's almost lunchtime and I don't want to put any more on Tiffany's plate."

My mom agreed. "Of course, Nancy. Go get you some rest. Spaghetti is easy. That doesn't take long at all. I can cook that and still have enough time to get my hair done."

Nancy said, "Good. I'm going down to the guest bedroom. The ground turkey is already thawed out in the refrigerator." Nancy closed the basement door behind her.

Suddenly, my arm began to vibrate. At first, I thought it was my phone, until my son laid his head fully on my shoulder. I started shrugging my shoulder to wake him up, thinking, "No. No. No. You don't get to just poop in daddy's arms and then take a nice nap. You better stay awake and deal with that funk like everybody else." My mom had already turned around to brown the ground turkey when the odor hit Tiffany. She looked up at me and smiled. I tried to pass him to her. But Tiffany backed up.

"No! No! You know it's your turn, Stu."

I grunted. "Fine." I told Roosevelt he could have a seat in the living room. Tiffany walked with me to our bedroom, not to help, just to lay down.

When I change diapers, I like to think I'm part of the pit crew for NASCARs at the Daytona 500. I'm always looking to break my records too. My fastest poop diaper is one minute and twenty-two seconds. My fastest wet diaper is fifty-one seconds. I laid Kendall across the changing table. I had all of my tools (new diaper, wipes, diaper rash cream, and grocery bag) organized and within arm's reach. I set my phone to stopwatch mode, took a deep breath, and then pressed start.

I ripped open the two latches and yanked the front of his diaper. Kendall's little wee wee was pointing straight up in the air and started peeing. A little bit got in my eye before I could back away. Not being able to see well, I just grabbed his legs and lifted Kendall's bottom so he could pee on the window. I yelled at Tiffany for help. "Engine malfunction! Engine malfunction!" Tiffany didn't even budge from her resting position with her back to me.

"Stu what are you talking about?"

"It's an engine malfunction! I thought I was just changing the tires!" Tiffany rolled over to look.

"What! Stu, just cover it back up with the front of the diaper."

"Oh. Okay. Thanks. I would've done that sooner but I couldn't see that good because it got in my eyes a little bit and I panicked." After that situation, the chance of me breaking my record was gone. But I was impressed with my son's range, though. He even managed to get some on the ceiling. The last time I saw liquid shoot up that far was at the fountain show in Vegas.

I walked back to the kitchen alone, leaving Kendall in the bed with Tiffany. On my way, I bumped shoulders with my mom in the hallway. "Whoa! Excuse me Mama. I thought you were cooking the spaghetti."

"I did. It's done now. You can go get you some. I left it on the stove in there." I looked down at my watch to confirm that only five minutes had passed since I walked in my room to change Kendall. My mom walked back to her room and closed the door so that Teresa could finish doing her hair. The kitchen smelled good too. But I've learned over the years not to get too excited about my mother's cooking until I've tasted it.

Although there was a serving spoon next to the large pot, I opted for a dinner spoon out of the drawer. I needed to get a sample before I decided to dig in. When I did, that one tiny spoonful tasted like spaghetti flavored Cheerios. My mom used elbow macaroni and didn't boil the pasta long enough. That was the crunchiest bite of spaghetti I'd ever had. Roosevelt came walking up behind me as I forcefully swallowed the spaghetti. "Hey Stu. I don't mean to impose or anything, but do you mind if I get some spaghetti? It's smelling real good right now, and I'm hungry as a hooker."

I jumped out of the way of the stove. "No. No. You're not imposing at all. Here, get as much as you want. As a matter of fact, let me grab you a plate."

"Man, thanks Stu. I can't believe ain't nobody else over here trying to get some of this good home cooking."

My dad yelled from the living room. "T-That's because w-we've already had her homicide...I-I mean home c-cooking!"

While Roosevelt packed his plate with spaghetti, he asked, "So what's up with that diamond y'all were talking about earlier?"

"Well, I wouldn't necessarily refer to it as a diamond. It's so small. It's more like a McDiamond. You know how you can have a mansion? But a smaller version is called a McMansion. Or how a small candy bar is considered bite-size or fun size. Yeah! That's it! Her diamond is fun sized. It just looks like some little mess you wear to let people know, "Yeah I'm engaged... I guess." Just wait til' you see it, Roosevelt. It looks like that boy went shopping in the mustard seed section of the jewelry store."

Roosevelt was outraged, evident from his reddish tone. He placed his plate on the island and pressed his hands against the countertop, while leaning forward to take a deep breath. "What! You can't be telling me my little girl is engaged right now! Not my Angel! That ain't happening! No way! No how! Who is the boy?"

I said, "Look, Roosevelt. You need to calm down. Nancy and Tiffany said that this happened to both of them and it's not a big deal."

"Tell me about the boy, Stu."

"Okay. Angel went to go pick him up and bring him here so we can meet him." I heard the screen door open and I glanced out the kitchen window to see Tiffany's car parked back in the driveway. I said, "That must be them at the door now." Roosevelt started getting antsy. He was bouncing around, punching his palm with his fist, and even growling. I had to put an end to that crap. He was making my dad nervous. He got bit by a dog before. "Hey Roosevelt. Unless your name is DMX, a grown man growling is weird."

"My bad, Stu. It's just been a while since I've had to beat somebody down."

"Roosevelt calm down. Nobody's getting beat down today. We're going to meet the boy and talk to him, that's all."

"Yeah, and if he ain't talking right, he's going to catch a beat down." I raised my hand to warn him.

"Um. I wouldn't be so sure about that, Roosevelt. I should probably tell you that he's a – ."

"Daddy!" Angel screamed as she ran over to Roosevelt and wrapped her arms around his neck with joy. "Y'all, I want you to meet my fiancé, Ratchet."

When that boy walked in my house, he looked just like I imagined. He stood 6'5" with shoulders as wide as my doorway, and dreadlocks down to his shoulders. Just imagine a body like Brock Lessner with a face like Lil Wayne. His gold teeth couldn't be ignored either because he was a mouth breather. He asked, "Hey Abigail, can I have a gallon of water?" As I looked around trying to figure out who Abigail was, I had a smile on my face because Ratchet had the voice of a 10-year-old chess player. Before I even knew what was going on, Angel emptied out a whole ice tray in the spare Kool-Aid container, and stood at the sink filling it up with water.

I scratched my head because all this time I thought Ratchet had a speech problem. I assumed he got kicked in the head one too many times and had an issue with slurring his words together. I figured since he butchered Angel's name, that he messed up by saying gallon instead of glass too. But I was wrong. Then I wondered, "What type of man messes up his fiancés name? What type of guest asks for a gallon of water…on their first visit? And what type of person sits around the house with a supersized Kool-Aid pitcher full of water, like that's normal?"

Roosevelt tried to intimidate Ratchet as he stared in his eyes and squeezed his hand while shaking it. When Ratchet squeezed back, I watched an uncontrollable tear fall from Roosevelt's face out of pain. When it was my turn to shake Ratchet's hand, I just gave him a pound. I need my hands. I still have to cook myself something to eat.

Angel walked over and handed Ratchet the gallon of water he'd requested. I should've charged him for that water too. I know I'll have to replace my Brita filter now. It was already starting to blink. I raised the question. "So how long have y'all been dating now?"

Ratchet scratched his head. "At least a year now."

Angel put her head beneath his arm, and placed her hand on his stomach with an uncontainable smile. "No. It's only been three months, Ratchet."

"Oh. My bad, Ava. It just feels like it's been forever."

I said, "It's been so long that you forgot her name, huh?"

Angel said, "No, Mr. Stu. Ratchet knows my name. He's just being silly is all. Isn't that right, baby?" Ratchet leaned down and kissed Angel's for head.

"Of course, Angie."

Roosevelt was so heated he used his fingers to rub the temples of his head. "So how did y'all meet?"

Angel and Ratchet went back and forth until she insisted that he answer. I used that time to read Ratchet's tattoos since he was wearing a dingy white beater. I couldn't make them out, though. His skin was so dark. It was like trying to see a star that was located in front of the moon. Ratchet said, "Yeah, so yo I was walkin' to the library like I usually do. And – ."

Roosevelt interrupted. "There's one good thing about you, finally. So you like to read and hang out at the library, huh?"

"Nah. I just go there to rent video games and DVDs for free."

Roosevelt turned around with his hands on his hips and looked up at the ceiling. My lips were quivering trying to hold back my laughter. I said, "Go ahead with the story." Ratchet continued.

"Yeah, so yo that's when I noticed that she was taking up two spots in the perverted parking."

I cut in. "I think you mean perpendicular parking."

"Yeah. Yeah yo that's it. So I ended up straightening out her ride and she straightened me out by passing me them seven."

Roosevelt walked over, snatched Angel by the arm and pulled her away from Ratchet. "Angel, I want to talk to you in your room, alone, now."

Angel argued. "What's wrong dad? Can't you see we're in love?" Roosevelt tried to talk some sense into her.

"Angel, the only thing that boy has going for him is that he's a mechanic!" Ratchet raised his long arms.

"Why does everybody keep thinking I'm a mechanic? I'm not a mechanic."

Roosevelt said, "Angel, the boy ain't even a mechanic?"

Angel said, "It doesn't matter what he does. As long as we keep loving each other we will be fine. Isn't that right, Ratchet?" Ratchet agreed.

"That's right, Anita."

Roosevelt lost it. "Look! Her name is Angel! Okay? Angel! I'm the one who named her so get it right! And what do you do for a living anyway?"

"I'm a UFC fighter." Roosevelt took a step back. "What's your record?"

"Right now, I'm undefeated. I haven't had a fight yet." I stopped everything.

"Hold up! Angel told me you had a bunch of knockouts!"

Ratchet waved his hand. "Those were all bar fights and gossip, not official UFC matches."

I just couldn't believe it. "What about the agent she mentioned that told you you had champion potential?"

"Oh yeah. That's my dad, Big Money Martin. He's always supported anything I do."

Roosevelt asked, "How long have you been training for UFC?"

"Well yesterday was my second practice, but I'm a fast learner."

I didn't mean to say this, but it slipped out. "Uh, so pretty much you're unemployed."

Ratchet was obviously offended as he rushed to respond. "No. I'm not unemployed. I have a fight scheduled for next month, if I win I'll get $10,000."

I said, "What if you lose?"

"I get nothing." No words came out of my mouth this time. But I was thinking unemployed thoughts.

As Roosevelt walked a reluctant Angel to her room, he met and passed my brother, Shane Jr. in the hallway. I got a whiff of the Black & Mild scent as Shane Jr. walked past the kitchen to take a seat in the living room. Ratchet and I went to sit on the couch across from my brother. We joined my dad and Frank in watching a college football bowl game.

I introduced Ratchet to the three of them, and immediately after he began texting. The timing was awkward, so I asked, "Is everything all right?"

"Yeah. I'm just texting my dad to come pick me up."

I said, "Big Money Martin, right?"

"Yeah. I was going to stay for dinner but it don't seem like Anna's dad is feeling me too tough."

"Angel."

"Oh yeah. My bad. But that dude is mad enough to want to hurt me. Trust me, I've been through this already with my baby mama's people." My dad busted out laughing.

"Th-this is just g-getting better and b-better!" Frank set up fast in disbelief of what he'd just heard. But he remained seated and raised his shot glass in the air to balance it after realizing he almost spilled his drink. Outraged, I stood up.

"What? Ratchet, Angel ain't ever say nothing about you having kids!"

Ratchet stood up too. "Yeah I do."

I sat down with my legs crossed. "Oh. Okay. Just making sure I heard you right."

Shane Jr. popped up with an enthusiastic smile and walked over to Ratchet. "Boy let me shake your hand! I knew there was something I liked about you! I'm so happy to not be the only person with garnished wages in this house anymore, I don't know if I should hug your help you."

My dad blurted out, "Help!"

I said, "Yeah, Shane. He doesn't have any wages to be garnished."

My brother snatched his hand back from Ratchet while looking at me. "He ain't got no job?"

"Yet!" Ratchet forcefully answered for himself. "I'm getting paid next month." Shane Jr. smacked his lips.

"Aw hell naw. That ain't no job! If you only get paid once a month, that's welfare!" I tried to explain Ratchet's so-called occupation to my brother, but I couldn't get a word in. "Nah! Nah! You can't tell me nothing about this, Stu! I know all about welfare! Some of my baby mama's on it. I know we ain't in South Carolina. We're in Maryland. But welfare rules are international. Trust me, I used to know a dude from Hong Kong who walked around angry all the time. Then one time I saw him at the gas station on New Year's Day cheesin'. I said, "Man what you so happy about?" He said, "First da' mont'! First da' mont'!"'"

Ratchet explained. "No. I'm not on welfare. I'm a UFC fighter and I have my first match next month."

My brother looked at Ratchet down and back up again. "Oh okay. My bad."

Frank shouted. "Yeah that crap still sounds welfarish to me!"

My dad asked, "S-S-So how m-many k-k-kids do y-you h-h-have, R-Ratchet?"

Shane Jr. said, "Got dang, dad! I don't know how many he got. But he's gonna mess around and have another one waiting for you to finish your question."

My dad said, "S-Shane you can g-go p-play with fire a-at a g-gas pump as far as I-I'm concerned."

"I got about one or two." Ratchet said as all the other men in the room nodded their heads.

They all made me feel so stupid for asking, "How can you have one or two kids?" But I just had to know.

Ratchet said, "Well I'm waiting on the blood test results to come back in for one of them."

They all gave verbal approval. "Oh I understand."

"B-Been there, d-done that."

"Fa sho'." I was so confused, I think my eyebrows were touching each other. My brother noticed the look on my face. "Look Stu. Not all of us have the luxury of being 100% sure which child is ours. That's why I tell all my kids the same thing. "I love you more than life itself. But I'm going to love you even more once the results come back.""

Frank asked, "So Ratchet, how did you and my granddaughter meet?"

"Oh, I was just telling them earlier that I was walking to the library when I saw Ashley double parked in the perpetrator parking." I didn't even try to correct Ratchet this time. I just let him finish. The worst part is that Frank, my dad, and my brother all nodded their heads while they listened, as if Ratchet hadn't said anything wrong. "So I walked over there and straightened her out. Then she slid me her seven." I'm so out of touch with the new slang, I had to look up "slid me her seven" on my phone to make sure he wasn't talking about anything sexual.

Once I confirmed that he was only talking about her phone number, I said, "Oh. Okay. That was nice of you to help her out Ratchet."

Frank stood to shake Ratchet's hand. "To a man, operating a vehicle is serious business. And parking is next to godliness. So the fact that you can just hop in a car at a moment's notice and whip it into place, makes you okay in my book."

Ratchet said, "Thanks. But I can't drive."

Frank snatched his hand back. "You can't drive?"

"Nope. I don't have a driver's license."

Frank took a step back. "You don't have a driver's license either?"

"Nope."

I said, "So how did you move Angel's car?"

"Oh. I just picked it up from the front and moved into place."

Frank grunted. "Em. I just remembered I need to go take my back pills." As Frank walked to the basement door, Angel ran in the living room.

6 | BLESSED

Roosevelt trailed behind Angel at normal walking pace. Angel crashed her head into Ratchet's chest and wrapped her arms around his waist. Ratchet grabbed her shoulders. Frank smacked his lips as he stood at the basement door. "Listen, Ratchet and Angel, I have to tell you both to your face that I'm 100% against you two getting married. Don't expect me to attend the wedding, the reception, send a gift to the house – ."

Ratchet interrupted. "I don't have a house, just an apartment… with a roommate."

Frank sighed. "You know what? Ratchet, to avoid you raising my blood pressure, I'm going to look at this octopussly."

Shane Jr. said, "Dang. You got a lot of eyes."

I blurted, "Optimistically, Frank!"

"If you know what I meant, what you correct me for, Stu? Anyway, Ratchet, I'm glad that you've surrounded yourself with someone who works. Because I know two unemployed people can't pay the rent. Hopefully your roommate's "having a job" ways rub off on you."

Ratchet said, "But he sells drugs."

Frank became inspirational. "So what? Don't *ever* limit yourself, Ratchet! You can accomplish whatever you put your mind to. Yeah, of course your roommate had to put in a lot of late nights and years of schooling to become a pharmacist. But there's nothing stopping you from doing the same thing." I was going to help Frank. But since he got on me earlier for correcting him, I decided to let him stand there and absorb the awkward looks of stupidity.

Eventually Roosevelt said, "Um, Mr. Frank, I don't think that a pharmacist would live in a ghetto studio apartment with an unemployed roommate called Ratchet. I think it's safe to assume that this guy sells drugs... *illegally*." Frank paused, then shrugged his shoulders before saying the number one thing that wrong people say.

"Well... you never know. But either way, I'm still against y'all two getting married! I don't even know what you want to get married for in the first place! Angel, have I ever told you what my five biggest regrets in life are?"

Angel answered, "No sir. What are they?"

"Jumping the broom, settling down, tying the knot, saying "I do", and getting married!"

"But granddaddy, all of those mean the same thing."

"Exactly. That's why you need to think long and hard about what you're saying you want to do. If anybody needs me, I'll be downstairs, asleep."

Frank went downstairs and closed the door behind himself. My dad asked, "So-so w-why *do* y'all w-want to g-get married?"

Angel's smile lit up the room as she looked up at Ratchet with dreamy eyes. "Because we love each other, and we want to spend the rest of our lives together, side-by-side." Ratchet scratched his head and looked back at the kitchen.

I asked, "What about you, Ratchet? Why are you rushing to get married so young?"

"Uh… you know… I ain't really in a rush to get married. I mean I care about Alexis – ."

Roosevelt nudged Ratchet's arm. "Angel man! Angel!"

"Oh my bad, pops. I mean, I really care about Alicia a lot. You know, she good peoples. She good peoples. But I'm all about taking life one day at a time. And in one day we'll be on our honeymoon. Angel spent her whole life holding out… I mean honoring God. And I put in… I mean *we* put in too much work to not get the reward."

Roosevelt charged toward Ratchet with closed fists. "I'ma kill him!"

Ratchet backed up and Angel grabbed her dad around the waist to keep him from coming forward any further. I said, "Angel get over here before you get hurt."

She cried. "No! I don't want my daddy to hurt Ratchet!"

My brother scratched his head. "Baby, if that's what you holding him back for, I don't think you have anything to worry about."

Angel slowly let go of Roosevelt's waist. I said, "Hey y'all need to take this outside. I'm still making payments on this furniture." Roosevelt cut his eyes at me.

"Outside? Stu we need to be beating his ass right now!" I stopped everything.

"No! *We* don't need to be doing nothing." My brother jumped in.

"Come on, Stu. You lift weights. You used to play football. Y'all can take him."

"Hell nah. Hell nah. Shane I'm not about to let you gas my head up with that preamble to a butt whippin' you just gave. Understand this; I exercise every now and again to stay healthy." I pointed at Ratchet. "That boy trains every day to kick ass! There's a difference."

With open hands, Ratchet extended both arms in front of him to warn Roosevelt. "If you attack me, I'll have to defend myself, pops."

"I ain't your doggone pops!" Roosevelt bounced around, in place, to hype himself up. "You know what, Stu? He only been training for two days. Besides, I don't care how much karate he knows. I'm crazyyy!"

Roosevelt ran toward Ratchet while yelling with his fists balled. He threw a hard-right hook aimed towards his face. Ratchet just leaned out of the way, grabbed Roosevelt's right arm, and slung him to the ground on his back. Within a matter of seconds, Ratchet had his legs wrapped around Roosevelt's arm as he pulled his wrist to lock in the arm bar maneuver. I thought, "Wow. Ratchet really is a fast learner."

Roosevelt pleaded with Ratchet. "Please don't break my arm! Please don't break my arm!"

Angel begged Ratchet, "Get off my daddy! Let him go!"

Ratchet calmly said, "I can't do that. He attacked me. This is what self-defense looks like, Amanda."

"Her name is Angel!" Roosevelt hollered.

Shane Jr. said, "Um. I really don't think you're in the position to be correcting somebody right now, Roosevelt. At this point, I think you need to just go along with whatever he says."

Angel looked up at me. "Do something, Mr. Stu!"

I thought, "This is some bull! Everybody wants me to do something now, after the fact. Roosevelt knew Ratchet does MMA. He was the one jumping around and hollering that he's crazy, like that's supposed to be a form of self-defense." Whatever I did, I didn't want to piss Ratchet off and have him break both our arms. Somebody needs to have both limbs to call the ambulance. I said, "Um. Excuse me, Mr. Ratchet sir. I sure would appreciate it if you let my buddy,

Roosevelt go. I don't think you'll have to worry about him attacking you again."

"You know, you might be right. But then again, you might be wrong. One thing I can guarantee though, is that as long as I hold him right here nobody gets hurt."

I wasn't expecting Ratchet to make such a valid point. I decided to ask the wisest person I know to speak to him. "Hey dad. Can you explain to Ratchet why he should let Roosevelt's arm go?"

"Y-yea. Hey hey now, M-Mr. R-R-Ratchet. I-I-I-."

Roosevelt screamed, "Oh hell nah! My arm will be broke by the time he's finished!"

I couldn't disagree with him. By this time, I was so sick of hearing Angel cry that I decided to take a chance and just physically separate the two. "Hey Shane. Help me pull Ratchet off Roosevelt." My brother ran to grab Ratchet's other arm and we both pulled. But he didn't budge.

In fact, Ratchet explained, "Y'all are just wasting your time. The arm bar is locked in."

Shane Jr. agreed. "Yea Stu! We just wasting our time! I don't see what the big deal is anyway. He got another arm."

Roosevelt screamed at the top of his lungs. "No! Please don't break my arm!"

Suddenly the doors down the hallway flew open and Tiffany came running down with Kendall in her arms. Teresa trailed close behind. Before I could even get a good look at Tiffany, I noticed that Ratchet had let Roosevelt go as they both stood abruptly to face Tiffany. She yelled, "What's going on out here?" That's when I saw why everyone stopped to look at her. She was obviously in the middle of nursing our son because one of her breasts were out.

I raised my voice and pointed. "Hey! You need to turn around and cover up! Your titties are out!" Tiffany got mad with me.

"Ahh! Stu how many times do I have to tell you that I am not a cow! They're called breasts, not titties! And I don't care who's watching! I will not cover them up until you call them breasts!"

I was so mad I couldn't even say a complete sentence. All that came out of my mouth was, "Put the nipple on the titty in the bra!" As I stomped toward her I kept repeating, "Breast! Breast! Breast!"

With her back turned to everyone, I held a giggly Kendall as Tiffany asked me directly this time, "What was going on out here?"

I said, "Ratchet and Roosevelt got into a fight."

"So you expect me to believe that me walking out here with my breast out brought an end to all of that."

I enthusiastically agreed. "Tiff, I think you're seriously underestimating the power of a titty...I mean breast. Shoot. Forget a fight. A breast can end a war. As a matter of fact, the government doesn't need peace treaties. They need pole dancers. Think about it. You've never heard about club being shot up...while there's a girl on the pole."

Teresa used this time to catch up with Roosevelt, who stood rubbing his injured arm. "Oh, hey Roosevelt. I didn't know you were here. It looks like you've been taking care of yourself pretty good after all these years, too."

Shane Jr. busted out, "What the hell!"

Followed by Tiffany, "Yeah, what the hell!"

Then I got pissed off. "What the hell!"

Teresa took a step back with both hands up. "Wait a minute! What the hell is everybody saying what the hell for?"

My brother spoke first. "You over here looking at him the way you're supposed to be looking at me! Have you noticed how much work I've been putting in to get some...I mean to get to know you?"

Teresa said, "Everybody needs to calm down. It was just a compliment."

Tiffany said, "No. I said what the hell after I noticed the look that went along with that complement too."

I said, "And I'm saying what the hell because I don't see why you should care, Tiff."

"I don't care, Stu. I just think it's weird and a little bit nasty. That's my sister and my ex. But trust me, Stu. That is so dead."

I said, "Good. It better be. Or I'll give Ratchet his first real job and hire him to start kickin' asses around here."

Without warning, we heard a horn blow from the front of the house. I peeked out the kitchen window and saw a man sitting on an electric scooter with a helmet on. He must've noticed me because he yelled, "Hey! Tell Ratchet, Big Money Martin outside!"

I relayed the message. "Ratchet. There is a man on a scooter outside named Big Money Martin asking for you."

Ratchet stood there with his arm around the shoulders of a grinning Angel. "Oh. That's my dad. I gotta go. And by the way, it's a moped Mr. Stu, not a scooter." Angel nodded hard, like there's a big difference between the two.

I felt embarrassed for Ratchet watching him get on the back of that moped and wrap his long muscular arms around his dad. So much so, that I closed the blinds and door completely. I didn't want people to know they'd come from my house. That might drive my property value down. I asked my dad, "What do you think about a man named Big Money Martin driving a moped?"

"T-That man is con-con-con-." Whenever our dad gets stuck on a word like this, in order to expedite the conversation Shane Jr. and I start guessing like it's a game of charades.

"Content!"

"Condensed!"

"Confined!"

"Confused!" My dad raised his index finger to acknowledge my brother's answer.

Still rubbing his arm, Roosevelt said, "I'm going to go ahead and get out of here too. I need to go check in the hospital… I meant hotel. Angel, I love you and I'll be back tomorrow morning. Angel ran over to hug her dad before he left.

— ✦ —

A few hours had passed and it was now time for us to be heading to church. Angel had already left to go to the club nearly an hour ago. Her outfit was tighter than a Republican budget too. But as soon as I said something, Tiffany and Teresa went on and on about how she's 18 now and that's how young women dress in the club. Even though I disagreed, I was willing to give up the argument in return for Angel promising me that Ratchet would not be with her tonight. Angel promised.

Everyone was dressed and ready. We stood in the living room waiting for my mom to come out. I was standing near the front door when I heard her bedroom door open. My mom walked out to the edge of the kitchen for everyone to see her. "How do I look?"

I don't remember what outfit she had on, what shoes she was wearing, or even if she was smiling or not. All I remember seeing were those 1993 finger waves my mom had in her hair courtesy of Teresa. The worst part about them is that they pointed straight up in the air. My mom's hair was higher than my rent. She looked like a black cone head. I didn't know waves could go that high. Now I know what a tsunami looks like.

I ran over to cut the ceiling fan off so that it wouldn't damage my mom's hair. I overheard Shane Jr. tell our mom while looking at Teresa, "You look great Ma. Teresa did a good job with your hair. Shoot. If I had hair I would let her do mine."

After my mom thanked him, Teresa said, "Oh. Shane, you and the kids should fly over to California and I can do your daughter hair."

Shane Jr. said, "Daughters. Plural. Either way, I don't want to do that again. The last time I flew with all my kids somewhere we had to charter a plane. And that took a big chunk out of my savings." Teresa slowly nodded. My dad looked up at my mom's hair, reluctantly grabbed her hand, dropped his head and shook it.

He mumbled, "D-d-drive me to d-drink."

I opened the front door to leave and was startled. Through the screen door there was a man who stood on my front porch in a black suit. His arms were extended with his back toward me as he faced a shiny black hearse parked on the street. I thought, "Lord you said you were coming back like a thief in the night. But I didn't think you meant *to*night." My first reaction to any random person standing on my front porch would be yelling. But I was so nervous that this might be my time, I figured I might get a few heavenly points by being polite. "Um. Excuse me sir. Can I help you?"

"Mop in the bucket! What's going on nephew?"

"Uncle Al!"

We hugged and then he came in and greeted everyone. As soon as he saw my mom, he said, "Whoa! What did you do to your hair, Samantha? It's a good thing we're going to church and not a movie theater. You might've got yo' ass whipped by the person behind you." My mom just laughed him off. "But I have to tell y'all. I saw something even crazier than that on my way over here. There was this real big strong dude riding on the back of a moped with another man driving. The tires were squeaking and everything!"

My brother said, "That big dude was Angel's boyfriend, Ratchet. And the guy driving was his dad, Big Money Martin."

Uncle Al asked, "A man called Big Money Martin drives a moped?" Everyone shamefully dipped their heads to agree. "Well with a nickname like Ratchet, at least the boy has a good job as a mechanic. That's something I know about firsthand."

Frank said, "First off, that's not something you know about firsthand, Al. You've been fired from every job you've ever had as a mechanic. Secondly, that boy ain't a mechanic either."

Uncle Al asked, "So what's his real name then?"

I said, "I don't remember. But it should be Recession since he's unemployed." I switched gears. "I don't want to talk about him anymore, though. It makes me upset just thinking about it. Uncle Al, I'm glad you're here. I didn't think you were going to make it. We're about to leave without you."

"Yeah. Sorry about that nephew. We had to do a drive by funeral up in Silver Spring, MD."

Everybody looked confused by his comment. Even Kendall had his drooling mouth open. My dad asked, "Al, w-what the h-hell you t-talkin' bout'?"

"Oh. That's my new business I was trying to tell you about over the phone, Stu. I'm done with being a mechanic now. It's all about Al's Pall Bearing Services." Uncle Al reached in his pocket and started handing out business cards. "So pretty much, when old ass people die they ain't got no young friends to be the pall bearer, and their offspring is too emotional. They're liable to drop their old ass way before it's time to. That's where Al's Pall Bearing Services come into play. They call us. We show up to the funeral and get it done, for a small fee of course. Or like today, we were driving by a funeral and saw some old, ancient looking man struggling with the casket. He slipped me $50 and I filled in for him. We call those drive by funerals."

Nancy asked, "Al, who is we?"

"Me and my wife, Tammy."

My mom said, "Al I don't think my baby sister is strong enough to be lifting no caskets."

"Yea right! As hard as she slapped me after she found out I was unemployed again? I beg to differ. I got off that floor, looked her in the eye and said, "You'll make a hell of a pall bearer."

I got excited. "Wait a minute! Aunt Tammy's here?"

"Yeah. She's out there in the car. She didn't feel right coming in after everything that happened last time between her and Tiffany."

Tiffany spoke up. "She doesn't have to worry about that. That's water under the bridge. That crap happened years ago." I ran out to the front porch and waved Aunt Tammy to come in.

Once Aunt Tammy got in the house she stood with her back to the front door. Her hands were crossed in front of her as she held her nose up in the air. Aunt Tammy looked about as comfortable as a Muslim in a barbecue pit. Although polite, her comments had underlying insults. "I love y'all's house. It's so quaint and cozy. The starter furniture y'all used to decorate it is cute too." Which in translation means she thinks our house looks small and cheap. Aunt Tammy lost it when she saw the baby, though. "Oh my God! Is that my little nephew?" Tiffany let my aunt hold him.

Uncle Al said, "I don't know why y'all named that boy Kendall. Y'all millennials got to go and make everything have multiple functions. It ain't good enough to just be a tablet no more. It got to be a tablet and a human now, huh?"

I said, "No, Uncle Al. We didn't even come up with the name."

Nancy asked. "So who named him then?"

Tiffany said, "Technically, Angel did."

Aunt Tammy said, "Oh, y'all listen to your kids. That's very white of you… I mean nice of you."

I said, "Look. One day a few years back, before we were even pregnant with Kendall, the three of us were out at lunch. I asked Angel, "If you had a little brother what would you want his name to be?" She said, "Kendall." I laughed because in my mind I knew there was no way I was going to name my son Kendall. But after a while it grew on me, and here we are."

Aunt Tammy said, "Yeah and I've had some hair grow on me since then too. But you don't hear me calling my kids nappy, do you? Either way, what's important here is that y'all have a beautiful, healthy baby boy. It's like God took the best features from both of y'all and made him… he looks just like Stu too."

Tiffany smacked her lips. "Okay Tammy. I'll take Kendall back now. We need to be leaving for church now anyway."

Beneath her breath Nancy said, "Water under the bridge my ass."

—◠—

I've never been happier to arrive at church in my life. My brother and Teresa decided to ride with us. We had to listen to them profess their ghetto love for one another the entire trip. I can only imagine what they would've did of Kendall wasn't strapped in his car seat between them. As we walked through the parking lot toward the front doors of the church, Teresa and Shane Jr. started patting themselves down like they were about to go through a metal detector. I turned around. "Hey. I know it's nighttime. But this ain't a club. It's church. Don't worry. They're not going to frisk you."

Teresa said, "Um. Obviously. We know that Stu."

Shane Jr. said, "Yeah, Mop In The Bucket. We lookin' for the last Black & Mild we just freaked."

I couldn't have cared less about that Black & Mild. So I walked in the church with the rest of my family. We were greeted by a pleasant female Usher. "Hey brother Stuart. You've got the whole family with you today, huh?"

I said, "Yeah. I guess so."

Now I see what it feels like to be in a rap group. Every member of my family felt like they had to personally speak to the usher for themselves. By the time she walked us in, the only row available with exception to the two rows up front reserved for the clergy, was in the far back. The usher raised her arm to seat us in the back row when my mother-in-law, Nancy flipped a switch and turned into Shirley Caesar on us. "By the grace of God the devil is a lie! Rosa Parks was my cousin. We're sitting up front." There was nothing the ushers could do. Nancy and the rest of my family walked right down the middle aisle as pastor was preaching. They held their heads high and didn't even put up an index finger or anything.

When Uncle Al passed me he mumbled, "That's where we supposed to be sittin' anyway." With his bubble coat still on, I bounced Kendall on my chest while apologizing to the usher. Then I went and joined my family in the clergy section.

I sat at the end of the row closest to the middle of the church. Kendall was in my lap drooling his life away and trying to put his fingers in my mouth. Not a minute could've passed before Angel came and squeezed herself between my brother and me to sit. I said, "Whoa. You showed up earlier than I expected. To be honest, I didn't think you were going to show up at all."

Angel put her arm around my neck and squeezed. "I know. Thank you for everything, Mr. Stu. You were so right. Ratchet was a jerk. All he wanted to marry me for was sex. I must admit, I lied when I said that he wouldn't be going out with us tonight. I drove to his place to pick him up and he invited me in. When I walked in he was all over me. He wouldn't take his hands off of me. He kept saying, "Let's start the honeymoon now." I told him no and he got all upset. He said, "I don't want to get married if I can't sample what I'm getting married to. How do I know if I'm going to like it?" That's when it clicked that he didn't care about me at all. So I ran to my car and drove straight here. Ratchet tried to chase me down with his father's moped. But it only goes 15 mph."

I reached over Kendall to hug Angel and kiss her forehead. I told her how proud I am of her. I also said, "Don't worry. You will know the right one when he comes along because he will be willing to wait."

Uncle Al, who sat directly behind me, tapped me on the shoulder. I passed Kendall to Angel so that I could turn to see him. Uncle Al whispered, "Stu, where's the body at?"

"Oh, I just handed him to Angel."

"Huh? What you talking about, Stu? Focus. There's usually a casket or urn at these things for me to carry. If I ain't carrying nothing, I can't get paid." My uncle almost made me curse in church.

"This ain't a funeral, Uncle Al."

"What? This ain't a funeral? Well what is it then?"

"It's my son's dedication to Christ and a New Year's Eve service. I told you we were going to church for the christening and then going to see the ball drop. What made you think that there would be a funeral at church?"

Uncle Al looked down silently and scratched his head to wonder. "Oh, I didn't hear that christening part."

Aunt Tammy leaned in. "Stu, you have to forgive your uncle. Ever since he started this pall bearing business he thinks that everything has to do with a funeral. The other day I cut somebody off in traffic because I was in a hurry. The guy rolled down his window and your uncle thought he screamed obituary. What the man really said was – ."

"No. No. It's okay, Aunt Tammy. I figured it out. Remember we're in church now. We're in church."

Suddenly I heard, "Zoom! Zoom!" come from the overhead speakers in the sanctuary. The words caused my pastor and stop preaching, and had the entire congregation looking around to see where it was coming from. I recognized the voice. So I looked up at the baptism tub behind the pulpit. Sure enough, there was my son playing with his rubber ducky and echoing, "Zoom. Zoom." into the microphone attached to the side of the tub.

I cut my eyes at Angel. "I thought I told you to hold your little brother?"

"I couldn't. He kept moving while I was trying to text Ratchet back. He keeps sending me apology texts. So I just set Kendall on the floor for little while. He must've crawled up there."

I snatched Angel's phone away and tried to crush it with my bare hands. But I didn't realize how sturdy those things are. So I just cut it off and put it in my pocket for later. Tiffany and I ran up to grab Kendall from pastor after he'd lifted him out of the empty tub. Pastor said, "Don't worry about it, brother Stu. I already took a break from preaching. Go ahead and call your family to the pulpit and we can get started with the dedication." As I waved for my family to come up, I heard our pastor tell Kendall, "You know you made the wrong sound baby Kendall. Ducks say quack quack."

Kendall looked up at pastor, dropped some drool on the microphone and said, "Zoom. Zoom." That made pastor laugh.

Pastor held our son up in the air and said to the congregation, "Tonight we will be dedicating baby Kendall to Christ."

One of the members of the church said, "Amazon got em' on sale for $39.95." Everyone laughed, including some of my family. I didn't turn around to see who, though.

When pastor took my son's coat off and handed it to me he said, "Whoa. Baby Kendall showing off his blessing, ain't he?"

I stuck my chest out thinking, "Yeah. That's my boy."

My brother looked at Teresa. "Yeah. It runs in the family."

Tiffany grabbed the baby from pastor. "That can't be true. Let me see." Her comment made me tuck my chest back in my shirt.

After digging in his diaper, Tiffany pulled out a janky looking cigar. Pastor took it from her, held it in the air and said, "Oh. It looks like somebody been freakin' a Black & Mild." I turned to see Shane Jr. and Teresa shamefully take two steps back. Pastor handed the cigar to his most trusted deacon, who just happened to have the blackest lips in the sanctuary, to get rid of it.

My brother smacked his lips and whispered. "Dang. That was the last one too."

Tiffany passed Kendall to me based on the pastor's instructions. He explained that because I am the man in the family that makes me the leader, not only in the physical sense, but more importantly in the spiritual. Kendall's chest rested against mine. Tiffany laid her hand on his back. Pastor told the congregation and family to point their hands toward us before he placed his hand on Kendall's head. I hadn't had this many people point and snicker at me since the last time I applied for loan.

Pastor began. "Lord we humbly come to you this evening to dedicate the life of Kendall Jones. We ask that you keep him covered with your blessings and protection. Lead him to walk in your will for the rest of his life, always seeking to know you better. We claim him to be a leader and not a follower from this day forward. Let him not give in to peer pressure, promiscuity, or greed. Lord let your light shine in him, through him, and onto others who come in contact with him. We also ask that you give his parents patience, because it is not easy to raise a leader. Keep them on one accord to serve as an example. Let them not to lean to their own understandings and the trending ways of the world. But give them the faith to raise their son according to the teachings in your word and consistent prayer.

Lastly, bless the entire Jones family to support Kendall's walk with Christ, and his parent's Christian teachings. Let it be that the whole Jones family, even the ones not under the sound of my voice, be blessed with 100% health, strong marriages, financial freedom, and prosperity that carries down to all of the generations to come. I rebuke any and every generational curse that keeps them from walking in your will and receiving the full blessings you have in store for them. Remove the spirits of self-doubt, laziness, alcoholism, depression, drug use, debt, poverty, obesity, unhealthy diets, unemployment, unfaithfulness, and divorce. In all these things father I ask that you keep this family the close knit, loving family that they've always been. It's in your name that we pray and give thanks. Amen."

With tears effortlessly flowing down my face, I looked down at my son. He stared back into my eyes, and for the first time uttered the word, "Dada."

From the Author

—⁓—

Thank you so much for reading my Family Holiday Comedy Trilogy. Your support is greatly appreciated. These comedic novels have been so much fun for me to write, and I'm glad to have had the opportunity to share them with you. However you celebrate, I hope that you enjoy your holidays this coming season. Thank you again.

INSTAGRAM – @TheWriterSJ

TWITTER – @TheWriterSJ

www.ingramcontent.com/pod-product-compliance
Lightning Source LLC
Chambersburg PA
CBHW031517040426
42445CB00009B/280